LEADERSHIP

Sara Miller McCune founded SAGE Publishing in 1965 to support the dissemination of usable knowledge and educate a global community. SAGE publishes more than 1000 journals and over 800 new books each year, spanning a wide range of subject areas. Our growing selection of library products includes archives, data, case studies and video. SAGE remains majority owned by our founder and after her lifetime will become owned by a charitable trust that secures the company's continued independence.

Los Angeles | London | New Delhi | Singapore | Washington DC | Melbourne

LEADERSHIP

PERSPECTIVES FROM PRACTICE

LAURA GALLOWAY

Los Angeles | London | New Delhi
Singapore | Washington DC | Melbourne

Los Angeles | London | New Delhi
Singapore | Washington DC | Melbourne

SAGE Publications Ltd
1 Oliver's Yard
55 City Road
London EC1Y 1SP

SAGE Publications Inc.
2455 Teller Road
Thousand Oaks, California 91320

SAGE Publications India Pvt Ltd
B 1/I 1 Mohan Cooperative Industrial Area
Mathura Road
New Delhi 110 044

SAGE Publications Asia-Pacific Pte Ltd
3 Church Street
#10-04 Samsung Hub
Singapore 049483

Editor: Ruth Stitt
Assistant editor: Jessica Moran
Production editor: Imogen Roome
Copyeditor: Neil Dowden
Proofreader: Leigh Smithson
Indexer: Adam Pozner
Marketing manager: Kimberley Simpson
Cover design: Jennifer Crisp
Typeset by: C&M Digitals (P) Ltd, Chennai, India
Printed in the UK

Library of Congress Control Number: 2021950702

British Library Cataloguing in Publication data

A catalogue record for this book is available from
the British Library

ISBN 978-1-5297-9343-7
ISBN 978-1-5297-9342-0 (pbk)

At SAGE we take sustainability seriously. Most of our products are printed in the UK using responsibly sourced
papers and boards. When we print overseas we ensure sustainable papers are used as measured by the
PREPS grading system. We undertake an annual audit to monitor our sustainability.

CONTENTS

DETAILED TABLE
OF CONTENTS

LIST OF FIGURES

LIST OF TABLES

ONLINE RESOURCES

Instructors can visit **https://study.sagepub.com/galloway** to access online resources designed to support teaching. *Leadership: Perspectives from Practice* is accompanied by:

A **Teaching Guide** containing teaching notes and assessment suggestions for each chapter.

PowerPoints for each chapter that can be adapted and edited to suit specific teaching needs.

ABOUT THE AUTHOR

Laura Galloway PhD is Professor of Business and Enterprise at Edinburgh Business School at Heriot-Watt University, Director of the EBS Incubator and joint Editor in Chief of the *International Journal of Entrepreneurship & Innovation*. She has a background of research in entrepreneurship, leadership and small business and has published widely in these areas.

INTRODUCTION

There are examples throughout history and in all cultures of how great leadership has facilitated great outcomes. In this book we focus on leadership in organisations and specifically on the contribution leadership can make to them. Leadership is a mainstay of organisational life. Whether in the public, private or third sector, the same principles apply: not only can leadership make the difference between good organisations and bad organisations, it can also make the difference between good organisations and great organisations.

In this book we will explore what leadership is and what it is not. The book also explores how our knowledge about leadership has developed over the years, and encourages readers to explore and reflect on how good leadership might be enabled in practice for the betterment of organisations and the people who work in them.

In each chapter of this book, knowledge is sourced from research and other evidence, and is supported by example testimony of how issues associated with leadership play out in real life for six individuals who are currently in leadership roles at various stages of contemporary careers. The six examples are selected from a variety of industries and national contexts to afford sight of a range of experiences that are nuanced by circumstances and sector. Each leader was selected for the book on the basis that they have been identified by peers and subordinates to have led well. That said, each also identifies challenges of leadership throughout their careers, and relates how they have learned and developed as a consequence and how they continue to advance their leadership ambitions and skills. Their testimonies are not facts and readers are invited throughout to critique some of the assertions made by participants. The testimonies do provide real-life scenarios and opinions, though, and they provide evidence of struggles and challenges as well as examples of some of the joys and other best parts of being on a leadership trajectory in real organisations. The six recurring leaders who provided testimony for this book are outlined in the summaries below.

LEADERS FEATURED IN THE 'PERSPECTIVES FROM PRACTICE'

Jannie Tam, founder of GROWDynamics, Hong Kong

Jannie Tam is the founder of the Hong Kong-based talent development company GROWDynamics. She has degrees from China and Scotland and a background of working and leading in media organisations, including US and Australian corporates such as Disney, Yahoo! and Dymocks. Jannie is a passionate advocate of lifelong learning and education and ethical leadership, and these underpin her commitment to develop GROWDynamics as a small and medium-sized enterprise (SME) specialising in leadership education for young people through to executives.

John Black, Fire and Rescue Service,* United Kingdom

John Black is a station manager with one of the UK's fire and rescue services. With over 25 years' experience, including different levels of operations and leadership as a firefighter, John has progressed through the ranks and is now the manager of three fire stations. This includes responsibility for local strategy and operations, including emergency responses and community safety and engagement, equipment, buildings and personnel. Within a rank structure, John has 16 direct reports who each have their own cascaded leadership roles, encompassing 250 people, including firefighters and support personnel such as administrators, maintenance crews and services staff, and these personnel maintain a consistent 24-hour presence and service.

Ken Lorenz, entrepreneur, United States of America

Ken Lorenz has a varied career as an employee and entrepreneur. Based in Albany in the state of New York, Ken currently has two businesses: a data analytics firm and a data analytics consultancy. Ken has lived in various locations in the USA and has worked in research, production, quality control, locomotive repair and software development. After a career in the corporate world, Ken started his own companies, including a distillery in Vermont and a discount travel firm partially based in India serving the US market. Throughout his working experiences, Ken has used data analytics to drive business goals and is currently working to help others do the same.

Claire McCarthy, Children's Health and Care Charity,* United Kingdom

Claire McCarthy is the Director of Operations and HR at a large children's charity in Cardiff in Wales. Originally from Glasgow in Scotland, she has worked in third-sector organisations throughout the UK, with missions including social exclusion, medicine, advocacy, international aid and famine relief. The Operations role includes the directorates of human resources, finance systems, donor communications and volunteering, and Claire currently leads a team of seven staff and supervises the activities of around 200 volunteers.

Victor Ikande, Hollins International Construction,* United Arab Emirates

Victor Ikande is a regional head for the construction firm Hollins, a US-headquartered multi-national company (MNC) with around 70,000 employees. Brought up in Nigeria, Victor moved to the UK in his teens and attended university there. Now based in the UAE, he leads construction projects in the Middle East, with a current portfolio of 21 projects at different stages throughout the region. Project teams can range from 5 or 6 people up to 70 or 80, including the inputs of personnel matrixed in from other departments (e.g. highways, services engineering, urban planning). Victor has oversight of all of Hollins' Middle East construction projects and directly leads two large complex ones himself, and these together involve leading 72 project leaders and staff.

Priyanka Thali, CACTUS Communications, India

Priyanka Thali is a managing editor at CACTUS Communications, a technology company accelerating scientific advancement. CACTUS has headquarters in Mumbai and regional offices in the USA, the UK, Japan, South Korea, China, Denmark, Singapore and throughout India, encompassing a staff of nearly 1200. Priyanka has degrees in psychology and journalism and joined CACTUS after university as a sub-editor, moving on to become an associate editor, a senior associate editor and now managing editor. She leads an in-house team of 8 in Mumbai and over 150 contractual and freelance editors and reviewers.

* Pseudonyms are used for reasons of anonymity and confidentiality.

The book will draw on the experiences of our six leaders through testimonies that are presented as 'Perspectives from practice' throughout the chapters.

BOOK OUTLINE

In each chapter of this book theories and concepts are summarised, and from there the links with and relevance to practice in organisations are explored. Each chapter includes sections that explain concepts *at their simplest*, and a set of questions to test readers' knowledge and to provide opportunities for reflection on practice.

Throughout the book, two recurring distinctions are made. The first of these is the difference between *management, headship* and *leadership*. While *management* is explained to be about organising, controlling and monitoring, *headship* is defined as having a role of authority and designation in an organisation. *Leadership* is presented throughout the book as different from both of these. Instead, leadership is explained as that which involves pioneering and insight and engaging and influencing others to contribute effort.

This leads to the second recurring distinction made throughout the book, that of the two core elements and functions of leadership: *thought leadership* and *leading people*. In this book, the practices required of leading that include envisioning, designing and planning, and imagining are defined as *thought leadership*. These are the kinds of activities we often associate with people who pioneer ideas, present new technologies, disrupt markets or other environments, and generally challenge and transform traditional ideas and ways of doing things. They can be in any sphere – political, artistic, literary; the point is that those who can imagine and progress a new agenda are identified as *thought leaders*. *Thought leadership* can include also the less spectacular, though, and in any leadership practice there will always be the need to envision and set goals and devise ways of achieving them. This is also *thought leadership*. The other core function of leadership is *leading people*. *Leading people* involves communicating with and influencing people so as to motivate and extract effort from them. Throughout this book theory and knowledge about *leading people* is explored and critiqued, arriving at our modern-day understanding that people perform best when they are supported to give their best efforts and when the outcomes of their efforts are of value to both themselves and the organisations in which they work.

Using these recurring conceptualisations – *leadership* (as distinct from *management* and *headship*), *thought leadership* and *leading people* – each chapter in the book explores leadership from a specific perspective, and within each chapter, along with the 'Perspectives from practice' of the six example leaders' experiences and opinions, readers are invited to reflect on their own experiences of leadership – as leader or as follower – in organisations.

The book starts by defining the terms and recurrent themes already outlined. It also explores knowledge and research on motivations and makes the case that understanding how people are motivated is critical in terms of informing leaders and developing leadership in organisations. From there, the book summarises theory and knowledge about leadership and how that has evolved over the years, and drawing from this, links with practices and experiences of leading in contemporary organisations are made. The book thus takes an approach that is both informed by and informs practice, but links that practice to theories and knowledge generated by scholarship and research-informed bodies of knowledge right up to the present day. As such, the book includes the most recent research and thinking about leadership, with a view to informing practice in organisations that will contribute to their preparedness for future opportunities, markets and other environments. Leadership is also explored as practice in contexts in this book, including the role of leadership in strategy development and in the example scenarios of projects, entrepreneurship, creative industries and high stakes emergencies. The book also looks at some of the most pressing contemporary issues affecting leadership in the modern globally connected world, including diversity, international and multicultural leadership and ethics. These topics are explored in some depth, again drawing from extant research and knowledge and linking directly to experiences and practices in organisations.

Diversity and culture are explored in order to shed some light and provide some guidance on how leadership might be optimised by being inclusive. In particular, the chapter on diversity explores the extent to which leadership in the past may have been limited by being less inclusive than it could have been, and presents some of the opportunities that organisations might generate by inspecting the types (and stereotypes) they tend to promote to leadership posts. Similar to this, the chapter on cross-cultural leadership explores how leadership needs to be cognizant of diverse staff and markets to be most effective. This includes leadership in organisations that operate in many locations throughout the world and leadership in organisations that perhaps only operate in one region or location but with diverse personnel. It also includes leadership in organisations that seek contribution from people of different ages and career stages as these too can be understood as representing cultural diversity.

The chapter on ethics is included since ethics is one of the most critical responsibilities of leadership and of being a leader. The rationale for much of the focus on ethics in the modern world is based on the United Nations' *Agenda 2030* and its associated 17 sustainable development goals. These have acted to increase the profile of ethics and focus the attention of governments and organisations in all sectors throughout the world to include ethical considerations – relating to sustainability, humanity, equality and equity – in their aims, their operations and, critically, their leadership. Ideas about ethics are explored in the chapter, as are complexities and challenges, from avoiding toxic cultures to protecting consumers and being compliant with regulations and legislation. One of the greatest challenges for leaders in the modern world is the requirement to hone their knowledge and analysis skills and to balance the interests of multiple stakeholders in an ethical way.

The last chapter of the book explores the central concern in many organisations of how structures and people may be best supported to enable leadership that may make the best contribution in the present and in the future. To this end, the book explores some of the latest thinking on how to develop people as leaders and how leadership might be developed throughout organisations. For organisations that rely on the work of others this is critical, and it is one of the things on which organisations spend greatest time and resources. And why? Well, to bring us full circle, because leadership – *thought leadership* and *leading people* – is the critical determiner of success. Whether small or large business, public or third sector, leading involves creating ideas and aims, and leadership is perhaps the most important means by which an organisation can achieve or even exceed them.

1
UNDERSTANDING LEADERSHIP

Pioneering, influencing and motivating

INTRODUCTION

Leadership has been the subject of debate and study for centuries. Indeed, according to one of the key scholars in modern leadership studies, 'there are almost as many different definitions of leadership as there are persons who have attempted to define the concept' (Stogdill, 1974, p. 7). This chapter will investigate some of these, and it will consider other related matters, such as what leadership does, why we need it, and how it relates to development for organisations and the motivations of the people who work in them. The chapter explores in some depth the distinction between *thought leadership* and *leading people*. It also explores how leadership, defined in both of these ways, may link to and be informed by knowledge about motivations. Before we get to these, though, we must first make the distinction between leaders, managers and the people who are in head or chief roles in organisations.

LEADERSHIP VERSUS MANAGEMENT

There is much overlap between the concepts of leadership and management. There are similarities of course, but they are not the same. A key writer on this distinction was Kotter. In a paper published in 1990, he attributed *planning and budgeting, organising and staffing* and *controlling and problem solving* to management, whereas he attributed *establishing direction, aligning people* and *motivating and inspiring* to leadership.

If we return to the two key elements of leadership, it is possible to see further distinction. First, *thought leaders* are those people who are engaged in visioning and/or pioneering (what Kotter calls 'establishing direction'). In this sense they are separate from managers because this is not a key function of management. Instead, managers may concentrate on organising activities and people so that processes are followed, but leaders are those who envision the need for the processes and sometimes create and resource structures and the processes within them. In terms of the other key element of leadership, *leading people*, leaders motivate, stimulate, facilitate, engage and coach followers. Alternatively, *managing people* involves organising, selecting, processing and monitoring the activities of others.

Here is a simplified way of looking at it:

- leadership sets and facilitates engagement with objectives to meet organisational goals;
- management meets and monitors organisational objectives.

In practice, it is clear that there is huge overlap between leadership and management. Throughout organisational life it is possible to see individuals who are in roles implying leadership, such as CEO, director, chief. There are also many cases where these same people do not pioneer ideas and have limited skills in motivating and engaging people. Equally, it is often the case that people who are in roles that suggest they have a management function, such as supervisor, project manager or line manager, can often exhibit great vision, great strategic and forward thinking, and may well be great motivators of people and influencers of practice. This discrepancy between the conceptualisations of leadership and management and what we often observe in real organisations in practice is confusing. To clarify, it is helpful to refer to the concept of 'headship', as shown in Box 1.1.

Box 1.1: Headship

In an article in the book *Leadership, Contemporary Critical Perspectives*, Ladkin (2019) uses the term *headship* to distinguish leadership as conceptually separate from any particular position in an organisation. 'Headship' also helps to explain the overlaps and the gaps between the concepts of leaders and managers.

Underpinned by reference to research by Kort (2008), headship is described simply as 'holding a position of authority' (Ladkin, 2019, p. 38). In and of itself, headship is not enough to suggest leadership. Ladkin explains it thus: 'merely holding a position of authority does not automatically make the position holder a "leader"' (p. 19). Headship does refer to power in relationships, but that power does not inherently suggest leadership. Leadership must *engage* rather than *coerce* followers, and so where followers are not engaged, logic dictates they are not experiencing leadership. Some people with headship roles in organisations may well engage and lead, others may not. Headship thus refers to a role in an organisation, but as we have all seen at some point in our lives, the concept of leadership is not always attributable to the nominal 'head'.

This leaves us with three distinct concepts in organisations: headship, leadership and management.

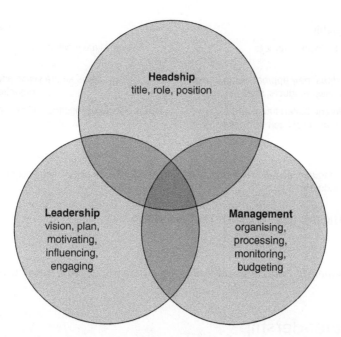

Figure 1.1   Headship, leadership and management

As Figure 1.1 shows, there can be much overlap between *headship*, *leadership* and *management*. The skills required of each is different, though. While *headship* signals a role, *management* is about monitoring, processing, accounting, organising and leadership is about influencing, motivating, visioning. In many circumstances these overlap, and in others they do not: many great managers just cannot envision or inspire and, indeed, some great leaders just do not have the attention to detail that efficient management practices often require. Thus, in practice good managers may or may not be good leaders and they may or may not be in headship positions. Good leaders, meanwhile, may or may not be good managers and they may or may not be in headship positions. Perhaps most critically for organisations, the aim is to have people in headship posts who have at least some ability in leadership, as explored in the next section.

DEFINING LEADERSHIP

It is argued throughout this book that there are two clear types of leading: that which involves *envisioning new ideas and solutions*, and that which involves *engaging people to extract effort from them*. These two key elements of leadership are referred to throughout the book as *thought leadership* and *leading people* respectively.

Thought leadership describes the practice of envisioning ideas and ways of doing things, pioneering and embracing development and change. *Leading people* refers to communicating those ideas and engaging and influencing people so that they contribute effort towards achieving their realisation. Figure 1.2 illustrates these as overlapping elements of leadership.

Thought leadership	Leading people
Followers may be local or remote.	Followers are local (or at least directly digitally connected.
Pioneers new ideas, new approaches to doing things, new process, products, services.	Advocates for the vision and values of the organisation or cause.
Envisions a different (better) future and communicates that, most often with passion and authenticity.	Leads people by influencing behaviours in context so that they contribute effort.
	Models and tools are useful for leading.
Pioneering and thought leadership can occur in any context or industry.	Leadership of people can occur in any context or industry.

Figure 1.2   The overlapping elements of leadership

The concepts *thought leadership* and *leading people* are unpacked a little further below.

Thought leadership

Thought leadership is used in this book as a term to describe leadership when it involves having a vision, deciding on an aim or a purpose or a mission, and then imagining, developing and planning a strategy so that activities required for achieving the vision can be carried out effectively. Leadership in this context can be about pioneering: having the independence in thought and imagination to conceive a different future, having ingenuity, having tenacity and having the skills to create a structure around ideas so that ambitions can be achieved. This *thought leadership* is therefore often associated with new organisations or change in organisations at either structural or strategic levels or both. Often we see the word 'vision' attributed to entrepreneurs and to highly successful transformers of organisations. Other common examples include the political world, where a leader's goals may include improving or at least changing outcomes for society in some way. There are also lots of examples in the scientific world and in the arts, where the ability to envision something new leads to development and creation and new ways of doing things. It is about pioneering and moving arts and science, understanding and ideas forward. But *thought leadership* goes beyond the spectacular and transformative, and includes too the practices of imagining, facilitating and developing in all sorts of more modest ways. For organisational life, in businesses, in public institutions and in third-sector enterprises, regardless of place in the hierarchical structure, *thought leadership* involves the same principles of envisioning, and so creativity and forward thinking, the ability to critique and challenge the status quo and traditional ideas, are all just as important. In organisational life, the critical factor of *how* aims will be achieved is required too. Often this involves the creation and development of structures and processes, and often it involves engaging other people to join you in this journey. This neatly refers us to the second element of leadership, *leading people*.

Leading people

When we think about leadership, the most common conceptualisation is that it involves engaging and influencing people. At its simplest expression, *leading people* concerns influencing individuals who are in some way following. This leader/follower concept is common in all sorts of areas. Many leadership texts and blogs reference leading in the natural world. It is common to see metaphors, analogies and even memes that suggest animals have somehow cracked leadership, from the V formation of ducks, to the king of the jungle image of the big cats, to the hierarchies of wolves, the alpha males of apes, the group-think of insects. In fact, as this short list suggests, in the natural world there is no consistency in terms of leadership – circumstances and context have determined how species have evolved, including how they lead. Indeed, some of the most popular conceptualisations are just plain wrong: a queen bee is less a leader and more of a servant hostage. Yet many of these ideas are projected into the human world and idealised. In this book we will explore some of the idealised images of leaders and critique them, but for now it is most useful to note that traditional ideas of *leading people* often rely on established wisdom that has applied in the past. That does not mean that this is appropriate for the future, and in fact, as we will explore in this book, most often these ideas are normative ideals only and are subject to much challenge; the most obvious example is that leadership looks like a tall, confident man in a suit, but of course this is based on the plethora of tall men in suits in leadership positions throughout history (men in military uniforms conjure a similar stereotype). It says nothing at all about competence or skills, or about whether and how followers may be engaged and influenced in modern organisations.

Leading people in organisational life involves influencing them in such a way that they engage and conduct themselves to the best of their abilities. It is about facilitating excellence, and having people provide best effort in line with the vision and goals of the organisation. In some ways it can be seen as manipulative. Essentially it is, but this does not mean that it is malevolent. Leadership works best where the interests of followers are congruent with the interests of the organisation. In the public and commercial worlds, people work in exchange for pay. But they do not only work for pay. They work for all sorts of other reasons too, including participating in society, achieving goals, developing and challenging themselves, learning new things, having an identity, feeling valued, being respected, practising talents and skills, meeting new people, making a contribution, having status. The list goes on and on and varies infinitely amongst people.

Consequently, old-fashioned stereotypes about leadership involving control and coercion of people are most often entirely ineffective in modern organisations (and pretty unethical, as we will explore in Chapter 8). Instead, good leadership engages people with *their* goals and aspirations in mind and links them to those of the organisation so that best outcomes are mutually experienced by organisation and person.

PERSPECTIVES FROM PRACTICE 1.1

Victor Ikande is a regional head for the US-based construction firm Hollins. More information about Victor can be found on page 3.

Jannie Tam is the founder of the Hong Kong-based talent development company GROWDynamics. More information about Jannie can be found on page 1.

Ken Lorenz is the owner of a data analytics firm and a data analytics consultancy, both based in the USA. More information about Ken can be found on page 2.

Claire McCarthy is the Director of Operations and HR at a large children's charity in Wales. More information about Claire can be found on page 2.

John Black is a station manager with one of the UK's fire and rescue services. More information about John can be found on page 2.

Victor Ikande in the corporate construction sector expresses the distinction between leading people and thought leadership thus:

> I have two heads if you know what I mean, where I'm delivering and I have to manage the team. But there's also that aspect where you have to set the vision of the project. We obviously have a corporate mission and vision, but what I have to do is to try to translate that vision into what it means for us as a smaller team ... You have to bring it down to what it means for your people. So in that way the vision-setting is your translation of the wider corporate mission

Vision was described as a critical motivator by the two business founders Jannie Tam and Ken Lorenz. Both identified that the thought leadership of the entrepreneur is the key attraction of working in a start-up:

> In a start-up, understanding the founder's vision is what gets people interested and motivated. They want to go work on that vision. No one wants to go work in a company where they're not sure what it does. (Ken)

> My staff came to me. I didn't actually have to recruit anyone, I actually had people coming knocking at the door saying, 'I want to do this, can we work together?' So I didn't find it difficult to find employees. But I think in this situation

you're not just treating them as employees anyway, because it's a small new venture. You have to have people with a bit of chemistry, but if they don't buy into the idea they wouldn't have come. (Jannie)

This idea of having to elicit interest and enthusiasm in a leader's vision is expressed also by Claire McCarthy and John Black in their respective charity and public sector organisations. Claire provides an example:

We had a really old-fashioned auditing system and actually I had a person who was really intelligent but she felt demeaned every single day because her work was given to somebody else to check and that someone else came through with a red pen and made her feel stupid. There was absolutely no need for it. I was keen to develop a new culture so I changed that and developed a new way of managing quality. As soon as people saw that the change meant that they were not going to be stuck in a room checking somebody else's work, which is the most tedious and boring thing you can ever ask anybody to do, they got on board because what we were doing would have such an impact on their working lives.

Perspectives from practice questions

1. What does Victor mean when he says he has two heads?
2. Why do you think both Jannie and Ken make particular reference to the vision being important in their organisations?
3. Why do you think Jannie has found it easy to recruit?
4. What effect did sharing the overall vision, including outcomes, have on the staff in Claire's charity?

Critical to understanding how to lead, whether in a thought leadership or a leading people sense, is an understanding of what motivates the people you need to commit effort to the work required in order to develop and realise the vision. In short, before one can lead and influence, one needs to have some appreciation of how people are motivated, and this is discussed next.

UNDERSTANDING MOTIVATION

The previous sections identified that leadership involves two distinct functions: the ability to imagine and plan for a different future, which we refer to as *thought leadership*, and the ability to influence people so that they give their best effort to the organisation, which we refer to as *leading people*. Before we can really understand leadership, we have to consider what and who is being led, though. This requires that we explore some key knowledge about how people are motivated.

The *Cambridge English Dictionary* defines motivation as a willingness or enthusiasm for doing something. As such, motivation is clearly associated with some psychological force whereby we are driven to action. Motivation as a psychological process is complex and there is a whole body of knowledge associated with it. For our purposes here, the focus is on how leadership may be informed by understanding how to influence and engage people so that their best effort may be drawn. As such, the next sections explore the broad ways in which people in organisational life experience motivation and how this may be used to inform leadership practice.

Extrinsic, intrinsic and pro-social motivations

A key way to understand motivations is to separate the distinct ways humans have been found to be motivated. For many years this was divided into two clear types: extrinsic motivations and intrinsic motivations.

Extrinsic motivations are those things external to a person that are required or desired by them. In organisational life, extrinsic motivations include need or desire for rewards such as pay, promotion, extra holidays or in-kind benefits, or the avoidance of penalties such as a pay cut, demotion or job loss.

Intrinsic motivations are those things that are less tangible but which instead speak to our well-being and satisfaction. In organisational life, these might include the need or desire for challenge, interest, development, learning, prestige. Many people feel their job or profession is part of their identity, and maintaining that identity is another intrinsic motivation.

Box 1.2: A word about prosocial motivations

Psychologists have long acknowledged that there is a third type of motivation: *prosocial*. Until recently, business studies have largely considered this as relatively unimportant since it refers to motivations to make social or ethical contributions, and these were assumed to be the domain of the political, social and domestic worlds rather than the commercial one. Recently, though, the world has become conscious of ethical and global issues in a way unprecedented throughout history (see Chapter 8). In part, this is attributable to the global communications we all participate in so people have become aware of the experiences of others throughout the world. Increased awareness and developing knowledge about international events and crises have amplified prosocial concerns further. These include what the World Economic Forum refers to as *Global Challenges* that we face internationally and as a species, such as securing sufficient food for the world population, addressing the climate emergency, mitigating gender and other inequalities, developing long-term sustainable economies, and more (World Economic Forum (WEF),

2020). While research institutes, universities and political leaders engage in these challenges, increasingly so do everyday people as well, and this feeds into the organisations they create and in which they work.

The United Nations (UN) crystallises some of the key concerns nations and the organisations in them may consider in their *Sustainable Development Goals* (SDGs). The implications of these for leaders in organisations will be discussed in this book again in Chapter 8. For now, though, the UN's SDGs are 17 prioritised targets set in 2015 for the year 2030. These are summarised in Figure 1.3, and are included here to provide some context to the idea that, increasingly, regular people are motivated by a desire to make a contribution with this type of ethos in mind.

Figure 1.3   The UN Sustainable Development Goals*

Source: UN.org (available at www.un.org/sustainabledevelopment/).

Theorising motivation

There are many different approaches to understanding motivation that have evolved and developed over the years. For leaders to influence people so that they may give their best efforts, it is useful to understand some of these. For the purposes of this book, a few key theories are summarised here to outline some broad principles for leadership. They are selected to exemplify and do not comprise an exhaustive list. The examples do, however, afford sight of some of the most established and referenced ways in which people may be motivated.

---

*The content of this publication has not been approved by the United Nations and does not reflect the views of the United Nations or its officials or Member States.

Expectancy theory

The North American business scholar V.H. Vroom came up with expectancy theory in his book *Work and Motivation* in the 1960s. It maintains that people are motivated to action if they expect their effort will be recognised and instrumental to the outcome and that the outcomes are personally valuable. It relies on the key components of *expectancy, instrumentality* and *valence* as illustrated in Figure 1.4 and elucidated further below.

Expectancy is not identical to expectation. Where expectation suggests hope and probability, expectancy refers more to certainty of opportunity. Expectancy theory therefore proposes that motivation is contingent on the belief or strong surety that contribution will be instrumental to personally meaningful outcomes.

Instrumentality refers to the effects of action, that action will cause an outcome. Expectancy theory therefore proposes that motivation requires that a person can make a difference or have an effect by their actions or effort. This effect may refer to benefits to either the organisation or the individual or both – the point is that action is instrumental to personally meaningful outcomes.

Valence means that effort has been meaningful and the outcomes desirable. It refers to the transposition of effort to outcomes that are valuable for the individual. This value may be emotionally or practically realised and therefore may be intrinsic or extrinsic – so in most workplaces, for example, it may relate to learning, well-being, etc. (intrinsic values) and/or to pay, promotion, etc. (extrinsic values).

In summary therefore, expectancy theory proposes that motivation comprises an expectancy that effort will be instrumental to outcomes and that these outcomes have valence for the individual. The implications for leadership therefore are threefold: that followers trust leaders (so that expectancy may be facilitated); that they are given appropriate tasks and roles in which to act (so they can exhibit effort that is instrumental to outcomes); and that leaders have some understanding of what followers value and find rewarding (so that these outcomes have valence for these followers).

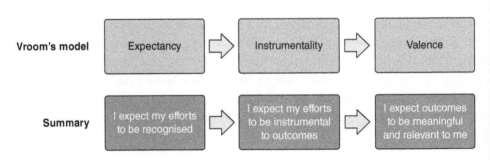

Figure 1.4   Vroom's expectancy theory

Source: Adapted from Vroom (1964).

At its simplest: Expectancy theory maintains that people are motivated where they expect that their efforts will be personally valuable to them.

Needs-based theories

There are several different theories that may be described as needs-based motivation theories. In the 1960s Herzberg developed motivator-hygiene theory, which proposed that motivation is contingent on meeting work-based motivations, such as challenge and professional development, and comfort-based ones, such as job security and sufficient income. This again recalls that drivers may be intrinsic or extrinsic for people, but in this theory they are presented as needs (Herzberg, 1966).

By far the most commonly referenced needs-based motivation theory is Maslow's hierarchy of needs. Originating in his book *Motivation and Personality* written in the 1950s, this theory on the psychology of motivation plots human needs on a pyramid in which these are prioritised from the bottom up, as shown in Figure 1.5.

The premise is that people are motivated to fulfil needs, but that needs are prioritised in a specific order for us as a species. Once a set of needs is achieved, we are able to move on to the next set of needs and we cannot move upwards until we have had the needs met. Not everyone will be able to achieve each ascending level of needs for a variety of personal, circumstantial and contextual reasons (hence the pyramid representation).

In sequence, hierarchy of needs theory proposes that people are motivated initially to fulfil their physiological needs for survival – the need to breathe and eat. Once these are secured, people are motivated to keep safe from predators and from harm and so require

Figure 1.5   Maslow's hierarchy of needs theory

Source: Adapted from Maslow (1954).

shelter and protection. Thereafter, once secure, people need to belong, to be part of a social grouping such as a family or community, and from there they will seek to develop esteem, profile and pride. The last set of needs to be achieved by those that have secured the previous building blocks are those referred to as self-actualisation. Self-actualisation is the sense of having achieved one's potential, to have fulfilled ambitions and succeeded.

The rigidity and generalisations of the key propositions in hierarchy of needs theory are such that there are lots of criticisms of it (the lack of flexibility to move about the pyramid is one key criticism; the representation of all of humanity within a model that evokes (male) Western individualist culture and capitalist structure is another). Nevertheless, it has been applied throughout psychology, sociology and organisational studies, including organisational behaviour and human resource management. For our purposes here, for leadership in organisations, the bottom two layers are often considered least important as it is assumed that these needs have already been met before joining an organisation. Again, though, this may not be true of all cultures and demographics, a critical issue relevant to intercultural leadership (discussed in Chapter 7). From there, love and belonging seem irrelevant on first sight too. In fact, though, this is one of the key ways leadership can be enabled in organisations. Rather than suggest that organisational relationships mirror personal relationships, instead organisational life can be viewed as analogous with family life. Where strong ties and emotional bonds link families, social interaction, familiarity and comradeship create communities in organisations. And communities and belonging are critical influences on behaviour – consider how unappealing an organisation would be if no one spoke to you, if others were hostile. Consider also how much effort would be exhibited if there was no sense of team or communal experience and if there was no consensus that effort was worthwhile, no role models. So belonging and community are important parts of motivation and are relevant to leadership. Similar is true of the top two levels: *esteem* and *self-actualisation*, and these resonate with ambition and success – again with clear implications for leadership in terms of influencing best effort. More broadly, the main implication of Maslow's hierarchy of needs theory for leaders is that it implies that leaders should endeavour to know where followers are in terms of their needs so that they are informed about how to cater for ongoing development within each level and facilitate an upwards trajectory where appropriate.

At its simplest: Needs-based theories maintain that people are motivated to effort when that results in the fulfilment of needs.

Other approaches to understanding motivations

There are many ways of exploring motivation. While expectancy theory and needs-based theories are amongst the most common, there are other approaches too. Goal-setting is one example. In a paper in 1990, scholars Locke and Latham consolidated earlier work and theorised that people are motivated by challenge and they seek to achieve goals. These may be set by themselves (intrinsic) or by organisations or other external bodies (extrinsic), but it is the goals themselves that drive behaviour, underpinned by an assumed achievement orientation.

At its simplest: Goal-setting theories maintain that people are motivated by goals.

Elsewhere, Adams (1963) proposes that equity is key. From a motivations perspective, equity theory refers to perceptions of fairness, both as a direct and as a relative concept. Therefore, people are motivated if effort is commensurate with output and fair. In other words, people are motivated where they see that there is a link between the amount of effort they make and the impact or value of the outcome of that effort for themselves, and that their efforts are relative. Consequently, in organisational life, equity theory would suggest people are motivated if their rewards reflect the extent of their efforts and the outcomes achieved by them, and that their rewards are relatively fair compared with those of others. As such, equity theory allows that people may be paid differently, for example, but this difference is based on some qualitative variance, such as expertise, experience or amount of work. If reward is seen to be unfair in either a direct or relative sense, motivation is reduced.

At its simplest: Equity theories maintain that people are motivated when there is fairness in terms of treatment and reward.

PERSPECTIVES FROM PRACTICE 1.2

Priyanka Thali is a managing editor at CACTUS Communications, a technology company headquartered in India. More information about Priyanka can be found on page 3.

Priyanka Thali explains that in her corporate publishing organisation people are motivated in a variety of ways, both extrinsically and intrinsically. While later chapters in this book will explore these much further, she notes:

> We try to pay attention to both the extrinsic rewards as well as the intrinsic. We do have incentives for both in-house people and contractors. We understand that at the end of the day ... people are driven by financial incentives. That's one side of it. On the other side, we try to get people to not only be motivated by these aspects; we try to get them to be motivated by other things as well. So one of them, specifically for in-house employees, is learning on the job and experience that they're gaining through that for career progression opportunities. And getting them involved in projects that they might enjoy. So we consider pay-based incentives important, but we try to balance it with the intrinsic as well.

(Continued)

In describing the way she has found young people in particular to be motivated in her training firm, Jannie Tam distinguishes between the value of extrinsic and intrinsic rewards. She notes that, for some, and especially in Hong Kong perhaps, intrinsic motivations can be the critical driver of work effort since extrinsic rewards can have diminishing value and can have limited ability to make a significant and meaningful difference to lives. She explains it thus:

> The trend is that intrinsic reward is probably equally if not more important than extrinsic rewards because the younger generation in particular always feel that life is too expensive anyway. Not many of them can really flourish just from a materialistic point of view. Everything is too expensive. Even if they work their whole life, they may not be able to live a life that is comfortable enough. It's just because Asia is very expensive and Hong Kong is super-expensive. So when you find it hard to fulfil your financial ambitions you pursue intrinsic ones. And even a pay increase I think is actually an intrinsic encouragement more than the actual extrinsic financial input because an employee probably cannot change their lifestyle by a small pay rise. But you listen to them about their personal aspirations, especially at this time for this generation, their aspirations of work, and try to reflect that in the day to day of what they do. [As a small firm] we can never compete with huge financial rewards, so intrinsic motivation is important and we have to think about why people would prefer working for a smaller company.

In his US business, Ken Lorenz notes similarly that one of the problems of extrinsic rewards is that they can only go so far in terms of motivating people. Resonating with the principles of equity theory, he makes specific mention of this as a limiting feature of working in the corporate world:

> The improvement in pay is never proportional to the work. So if you do just a little bit better you get a bonus, but if you do exceptional you get the same ... And I think where in the corporate structure you can only get one per cent raise this year no matter how hard you work, that limits creativity and effort. I don't think you can motivate people to do great things or to be exceptional with a one per cent pay improvement.

Instead, Ken notes: 'You have to have a reward system that is equated to people's values.'

In the charity sector, Claire McCarthy notes the common assumption that people are intrinsically motivated. She points out this is not always the case, though:

> Definitely some people are motivated by their salary and they think what they earn is reflective of status. Other people want a decent wage, they don't want to be underpaid, but actually that's not what will keep them at your workplace. What will keep them is if they're happy at work, if they like their colleagues

and if they're valued. There's not a huge reward system available but people, I've noticed, especially younger people, they like to be thanked. But basically I think most people in the charity sector do want decent pay now. It is vocational, but they want to earn well. It's seen much more professionally now than when I started – at that time it was almost like there was a perception that you are a good person and that was enough. But that's not the case now because charities are big business. We are talking millions and millions of pounds and you need people who know what they're doing and people know that and so they want a professional wage for what they're about to bring to the table.

Perspectives from practice questions

1. Explain how the extrinsic and intrinsic motivations described by Jannie and Priyanka in their organisations overlap.
2. Do you agree with Jannie and Ken that the (extrinsic) rewards structures in large organisations are limited in terms of motivating people?
3. Like Jannie, do you think younger people are motivated differently than older generations? If so, what do you think are the reasons for this?
4. Consider the motivations Jannie and Priyanka describe. In what ways do these resonate with any of the established motivations theories?
5. Why do you think Ken finds it easier to motivate in a start-up than in a large firm?
6. In Claire's testimony she refers to the importance of extrinsic motivations in the charity sector. Consider why this might be the case. What are the implications of this for the sector?

SUMMARY: DEFINING LEADERSHIP AND UNDERSTANDING MOTIVATION

In this chapter, leadership has been defined as involving both vision and influence. A clear distinction between these key properties of leadership and the more structured role of the manager is made, and indeed a clear distinction is made between leadership and the common practice of headship that is so often conflated with it.

The two key functions of leadership, *thought leadership* and *leading people*, have been explained as the practices of pioneering and strategising, and of influencing and engaging people to enable best effort respectively. These two functions are conceptually different but overlaps between them in organisational leadership practice are common. The pioneer may envision a future or organisational change, may plan it, set strategy and determine milestones. But he or she cannot achieve it alone. They will only achieve these if they take others on the journey with them. The way they do this can make the difference between achieving well, achieving satisfactorily or not achieving at all. In modern organisations people are unlikely to contribute time and effort in exchange just for pay. Indeed, when pay alone is the reason people show up in an organisation, then it is almost a foregone conclusion that their effort will be limited to the bare essentials. To engage people so that best effort may be realised requires that they are influenced and driven by forces beyond just immediate reward (or, alternatively, avoidance of punishment). With that in mind, this chapter has also provided a summary introduction to some of the ideas and theories that are key to our understanding of how and why people are motivated to act and contribute effort in organisations. Critical distinctions between extrinsic and intrinsic value are made with a focus on their effects on motivations. Some of the most prevalent theories of motivations are also summarised with a view to informing how leadership may engage with motivations to influence people and enable contribution in organisational life.

The rest of this book synthesises knowledge about how leadership can be developed so that practice may be optimised. It explores leadership as a strategic function requiring a pioneering spirit, and it explores how our understanding of leadership as an influence on the actions and efforts of followers has evolved. From there, leadership as practice is explored with a view to supporting development of leadership skills and abilities, including in different contexts and circumstances so that effective, inclusive and ethical organisations may flourish.

EXERCISES

Give an explanation of the two functions of leadership: *thought leadership* and *leading people*.

Give an explanation of the concepts of *management, leadership* and *headship*.

How do the concepts of *management, leadership* and *headship* help us understand practice in organisations?

Reflect on your own organisation: consider who are the heads, who are the leaders, who are the managers. Do these conform to the formal hierarchy?

What is the difference between extrinsic and intrinsic value or motivation?

Consider your own approach to your current or last job. To what extent were you motivated by extrinsic factors and to what extent were you motivated by intrinsic ones?

Consider some activity you choose to do often – sport or hobby or community work or domestic undertaking. What makes you choose to do this? What are the extrinsic or intrinsic value(s) you realise?

In no more than two sentences, summarise your understanding of the main theories of motivation.

Reflect on an organisation you are familiar with. How useful are needs-based, expectancy and other theories of motivation in explaining the practices there?

2
TRADITIONAL APPROACHES TO LEADERSHIP

INTRODUCTION

The way that we understand leadership has evolved over the years. Current thinking about leadership is far more informed, inclusive and comprehensive than it has been in previous times. Traditionally, in formal education, science, philosophy, society and business have been explored from a Western-culture perspective. Leadership has been no exception to that Western bias. But, of course, leadership is not restricted to any one region, type of person or even circumstance; it happens throughout human and social life. Increasingly, therefore, in all spheres, scholarship now engages with knowledge and traditions that have emerged from other historic and cultural sources and this has informed and enriched how we understand the world, including the humans who inhabit it. For leadership in organisations, though, since the traditions of neoliberal capitalism are Western in origin and have followed from pre-industrial and industrial modes of work, the traditions of leadership – understanding it and developing it – have followed a similar and parallel evolution. The development of knowledge in this tradition is the focus of this chapter, but it is important to note that leadership continues to be expressed in myriad ways throughout the world, and in organisations across the globe leadership practice is often informed by alternative traditions – a topic we will return to in Chapter 7 on leadership and culture.

For now, we turn to how the dominant paradigms of leadership and how our understanding of leadership in organisational life have developed during the modern historical period, and how research has informed leadership practice over the years.

EARLY THEORIES OF LEADERSHIP: THE 'GREAT MAN' AND HIS TRAITS

The first real analyses of leadership in the modern world were based on the idea that there is a set of traits that distinguish leaders. This emerged from earlier theories about human nature, and particularly 'great man theory' (see Box 2.1).

Box 2.1: A word about great man theory

'Great man theory' is a nineteenth-century Western interpretation of the world whereby history is understood to have been created and shaped by a series of great men and their actions. Emerging from the writings of the Scottish philosopher Thomas Carlyle in the 1840s, the great man is presented as a hero figure, and the trajectory and outcomes of humanity are the consequences of great men of history. Great man theory presumes innate talents and skills commensurate with greatness, even (in some writings) supported by divine selection (Carlyle, 1841). In the modern world, these ideas seem a little preposterous and this is largely because we have much more inclusive and scientific means by which we interpret and understand the natural and social worlds. We now appreciate that in all cultures and in all periods of history, the actions of individuals (great or not) are not discrete from the contexts and circumstances they are in – that other things beyond the agency of individuals are at play at all times and that these can be as influential as and are often far more influential than the actions of any one person in terms of shaping social life and history. Indeed, even in the nineteenth century, great man theory was criticised for its unilateral attribution of individuals to events and outcomes. Notwithstanding that, great man theory has at its core the principle that some people have specific traits commensurate with greatness, and this had an influence on early modern thinking and knowledge about leadership.

Traits are features of an individual's personality or character, and, as such, traits are parts of an individual's psychology. In modern psychology, trait theory has long been a core pillar, and since at least the mid-twentieth century onwards there has been much borrowing from psychology to apply to leadership.

In a book written in 1938, for example, C.I. Barnard wrote that 'executives' have special characteristics and abilities, such as intelligence, energy and resourcefulness, which differentiate them from others. Ten years later, in a systematic study of the traits of leaders, one of the most prolific early leadership scholars, Ralph Stogdill, identified that leaders tend to exhibit attributes such as intelligence, persistence, initiative, confidence, responsibility, social skills and insight (Stogdill, 1948). There are many other studies making similar claims, including recent ones, such as McClelland (1985) and Lord et al. (1986) at the end of the twentieth century and Yukl (2010) and DeRue et al. (2011) well into the twenty-first century. Amongst the traits found are intelligence, authority, initiative, resilience, creativity and even physical attractiveness.

Most of the studies of the traits of leaders in organisations have been conducted using psychology-based methodologies on the leaders themselves, such as psychometric tests and personality profiling. Interestingly, though, while a broad list of characteristics has been identified by these means, in the few studies that have asked followers which traits they believe are important in leaders, responses tend to identify the key elements of honesty, integrity and competence. In their book *The Leadership Challenge*, scholars Kouzes and Posner (2012), for example, report these are prioritised amongst followers consistently in studies they have conducted over many years.

At its simplest: Trait theory proposes that leaders have specific innate traits

Critiques of trait theory in leadership studies

In a study in 1993, the business philosophy scholar Charles Handy reported that attempts to identify a common set of traits amongst leaders are inconclusive and that there is no set of traits consistent throughout empirical researches. As such, it appears there is no 'formula' by which to identify a leader. Consequently, trait theory seems limited in terms of helping us understand leaders and leadership. And this is not the only problem associated with applying traits to explain leadership.

First, in most of the research studies that explore traits in leaders, the people being studied were defined as 'successful' leaders. In the earliest studies this most often referred to military or political leadership and the leaders studied were those who had won some sort of campaign. The 'winning' thus was how successful leadership was defined and, in turn, the win was attributed, at least in part, to their leadership. In fact of course, causality is not at all clear when we inspect historical and political life. Leadership may well play a part in successful campaigns, but so too do other things such as availability of resources, access to information, communication and developed technology (consider the effects on the geopolitical landscape that differences in weaponry have had over the centuries, for example). Following this, in studies in commercial and other organisations, all the people studied were already recognised as leaders. This means they had been selected and employed in roles with a leadership component and expectation. During the industrial and post-industrial periods, these leaders tended to have had similar types of background and education and similar access to resources and information. In addition, they were almost exclusively men, and indeed several studies identify 'masculinity' as a trait common amongst leaders! As a result, it is perhaps more accurate to say that what were studied were the traits of people who were in senior positions in organisations in a specific period of history, rather than any independent conceptualisation of leadership. In other words, at best, older traits studies tended to focus on the people who happened to be in '*headship*' positions at a specific point in history rather than true leadership.

The second issue with trait theory is that it assumes leaders are born and not made. Traits, by definition, refer to innate qualities that you have or you do not have in your personality. This evokes the idea that when it comes to leadership you've either 'got it or you haven't'. It suggests that since there are traits commonly associated with leadership, if you do not happen to have these traits you cannot be a leader. It also implies that leadership is not something a person can learn or develop. Beyond this, the implication that there is a set of 'correct' personality types for leadership suggests that some people have naturally occurring leadership qualities. On the flip side of this, the third criticism of traits theory emerges, though: if we accept that some people are innately qualified to be leaders because of their traits, then we implicitly suggest that some others are not.

The greatest issue with this third major problem of applying trait theory to leadership is its potential for disingenuous conflation with privilege and entitlement. The conceptual leap from *innately qualified as a leader* because of some combination of personality traits to *entitled to be a leader* is not a huge one, and indeed, throughout history there has been misrepresentation of the role of traits in selecting leaders and practising leadership. It brings us right back to the problems with great man theory in that it resonates with the idea that the 'great man' has an infallibility. It also suggests that if some people are born to be leaders, then other people (or other *types* of people) are not. This lends itself to a rationale that supports notions of hierarchy, entitlement and discrimination as legitimate – even the title 'great man' suggests leadership and success are male domains. These sorts of notions are incomprehensible by modern standards, and are even considered reprehensible, prejudicial and dangerous in most modern liberal cultures.

Trait theory and modern leadership

Despite the limitations, there is still much research that focuses on the personality and traits of leaders, and it is credible and contributory work. As we will explore later in this book, the traits of charisma, charm and sociableness in particular are all clear influencers of people (see Chapter 3). These are traits, and there are many examples throughout historical and contemporary life where there is clearly something about the personality of a leader that has facilitated and enhanced their ability to lead. Traits form *only a part* of the picture, though; in isolation trait theory is limited, but it does still prevail as an important part of our current understanding of leadership and does have an effect on modern leadership practice. As such, trait theory is not entirely redundant in leadership studies. However, alongside trait theory, other ways of understanding leadership were emerging throughout the twentieth century, and thinking on the subject started to associate leadership with skills and behaviours rather than with innate traits. It is to skills and behaviour-based theories therefore that we turn next.

EARLY THEORIES OF LEADERSHIP: SKILLS AND BEHAVIOURS

Even when conducting research on the traits of leaders in the late 1940s, Stogdill noted that traits alone could not explain leadership well. In a later work, Stogdill and Coons (1957) noted that while traits were important, there were also other influences on the behaviours of leaders, including their skills and knowledge. This marked a shift in how scholars of the time explored leadership, with greater focus on the behaviours, rather than the traits, of leaders. A seminal example is the 1955 work of Robert Katz, where he theorised three basic skills of leaders: technical skills (or knowledge), human skills (or social skills) and conceptual skills (ideas generation and development). The key advancement here is that, by exploring the role of skills and behaviours amongst leaders, leadership is understood not as something that is innate to a few individuals, but involves also things that may be learned. In addition, behaviour-based theories also allow that different types of leadership are possible because if skills and abilities vary amongst people, so too will the behaviours that are shaped by them.

Since early research that explored the behaviour of leaders, many studies have investigated different leadership behaviours. These studies are often complex and include research in multiple organisations and across geographies and time. Consequently, there are now many behaviour-based theories, some of which have been modelled and critiqued. In this chapter and the following one, we will mention some of the most commonly referenced models, but before we do it is timely at this point to refer to a review article by Mumford and colleagues published in 2000. In the article they noted that behaviours are informed by a variety of influences, from experience to formal education, and as such the development of leadership behaviours might be influenced by knowledge and explicit skills (such as understanding technology or an ability to problem solve), and by tacit skills (those developed by background, career and other experiences). These first set of influences – knowledge and explicit skills – require education, the second – experience – may develop over time. In both cases, though, the critical issue is that behaviour is influenced by external circumstances and this suggests that leadership is not entirely or absolutely the property of an individual, but instead is contingent on context and environment too.

Tables 2.1 and 2.2 summarise and paraphrase the basic principles that recur in behavioural models of leadership, whether older, modern or even present day. First, Table 2.1 summarises a tendency for behavioural models of leadership to split the types of leadership into two distinct sets.

Table 2.1   Task versus person leadership

Task-based – where the leadership that is required is focused on completing tasks

Person-based – where the leadership that is required is focused on developing people

Table 2.2 presents leadership behavioural styles. In some models four types are described, in others there are three or five. Here they are presented as four (with autocratic and directive leadership conflated).

Table 2.2   Behavioural styles of leadership

Behaviour type	Description and overlapping types	In practice in organisations?
Directive	'Command and control' and autocratic leadership are other (more severe) types of directive leadership. They rely on authority, power and compliance. Non-compliance can result in punishment. In all types of directive leadership, followers must follow specific procedures and there is little room for autonomy.	Directive leadership may be appropriate in manufacture and other tasks that require process and rules. Autocratic leadership may even be applied in emergency service organisations, and in other workplaces where health and safety risks are high (referred to as dynamic, high-stakes environments in Chapter 5). **Examples: assembly lines, food preparation, mine rescue, emergency response**
Consultative	Democratic and consensual leadership are similar. These describe types of leadership where there is either consultation with others or where there is consent (following consultation) to represent or decide on behalf of others.	Many projects and other types of team-working rely on consultative leadership. In any circumstances where knowledge and expertise and critical, including where innovation and creativity are sought, consultation and useful. Additionally, consultative leadership can be useful in terms of developing trust and in soliciting informed opinions on regular operations, and this too can afford combined knowledge and skills with the potential to generate new ideas and opportunities. **Examples: new product development, civil engineering, health and social care**
Supportive	Participative leadership is similar. What is described here is that people are supported to develop, requiring communication and relationships between leaders and followers (and, as such, overlapping with the consultative leadership described above).	Many people are keen to learn and take on new challenges so that they may develop personally, in organisations and throughout careers. Supportive leadership is observable wherever there are opportunities to advance. The rationale for supportive leadership is that as a person develops, so too does their value to the organisation and its goals. **Examples: any junior management or junior specialist role, such as commis chef, assistant professor**

Behaviour type	Description and overlapping types	In practice in organisations?
Laissez faire	*Delegative leadership* is similar and terms such as '*achievement oriented*' and '*management by exception*' also signal laissez-faire leadership. It refers to limited or no leadership, and leadership intervention only where required (by exception).	In many organisations professional people are left to get on with their jobs without direction or any specific leadership intervention. They are expected to have the skills to design and plan their tasks and execute them. In most cases laissez-faire leadership suggests a trust that people have the technical competencies and self-management skills required of the job they do. **Examples: teaching, accountancy, website and app development**

Many theories and models of leadership right up to the present day rely on the distinctions summarised in the two tables above. There is also much overlap between the principles outlined in Tables 2.1 and 2.2 – even on first sight, it appears reasonable to expect that tasks are more likely to be facilitated by directive and consultative approaches, whereas professional practice and innovation may be best facilitated by consultative or supportive approaches that enable and realise value from the development of the person, or even laissez-faire leadership. For each type of leadership and each orientation of it as either task- or person-based, different behaviours are implied.

At its simplest: Behaviour theories propose that leadership is exhibited by specific behaviours that may be informed by traits (and are thus innate) *and* skills and experiences (that may be learned or developed). Different behaviours are appropriate depending on whether the leadership involves tasks or persons.

Critique of early skills and behaviour theories of leadership

As for trait theory, the notion that there is a common set of skills and behaviours that will enable and enhance leadership evokes a similar idea of there being a recipe of behaviours to adopt if one is to become a good leader. Even when the distinction between task-based and person-based leadership is made, the implication remains that there is a set of behaviours for each. In an edited book on leadership in 2004, though, John Antonakis and colleagues asserted that throughout research studies over the years there has been no common set of behaviours found consistently amongst leaders. A further criticism of the earliest studies and interpretations of the role of behaviours in leadership is that, similar to trait theory, they implied that leadership resides entirely in the individual and took little or no account of the surrounding environment and context beyond the task-based or person-based orientation. Critically, though, this task-based versus person-based leadership distinction implies that context is important. Consequently, addressing this became central to the next generation of research that sought to develop understanding of leadership, where rather than being internal and personal, effective leadership began to be understood also as contingent on circumstances and context. We turn to this next.

CONTEXT-INFORMED THEORIES OF LEADERSHIP

Central to all context-informed theories of leadership is the idea that leadership varies depending on the situation. In the 1960s several theories were developed that, for the first time, included that leadership was affected by context and circumstances. Amongst early ones are Douglas McGregor's Theory X and Theory Y (McGregor, 1960), which models two types of leader, Type X and Type Y, most suited to either task- or person-based situations respectively. Illustrated in Figure 2.1, these types should be deployed as appropriate to followers and their aptitudes and engagement, with Type X having a directive orientation most appropriate for people who are lacking engagement and, depending on the task they are doing, need to be incentivised with rewards or penalties. Alternatively, Type Y is most suitable where followers are independent and engaged, and so can participate in a more consultative relationship with a leader.

Blake and Mouton's managerial grid (1964) proposes greater complexity in terms of types of leader behaviour, and identifies specific leadership approaches. First, these depend on the extent to which a situation is task-based or person-based. From there, leadership behaviour is plotted in a model that indicates the type of behaviours exhibited in different task- versus person-oriented scenarios (see Figure 2.2). The various types of leading are as follows:

- **The impoverished leader** where there is little concern for people and for task. This style is found amongst leaders (perhaps more appropriately called, heads – see Chapter 1) who have limited knowledge and skills in leadership and are protecting their positions and careers.
- **The country club leader** where there is concern for people but low concern for task. These leaders seek to make a comfortable and pleasant environment for followers where people get along. This makes for a good working culture but can have a limited impact on output and performance.
- **The authority compliance-oriented leader**, where the focus is on obedience of followers and penalty for low performance (a little like McGregor's Theory X type).
- **Middle of the road leadership**, where there is a balancing of the ambitions and interests of the organisation with those of followers. As such, there is concern for both people and tasks, but the compromise suggests a limitation in terms of achievability of support for people and for performance and outputs.
- **The team manager** has high concern for people and high concern for task. Potentially the best fit with the definition of *leadership* as opposed to *management* and *headship* (see Chapter 1), and similar to McGregor's Theory Y type, the team manager style of leadership

encourages consultation and developing teams that are both pleasant for followers to work in and productive.

Path–goal theory, first developed in 1971 by Robert House, is another contextualised behaviour theory. Path–goal theory uses the task–person distinction, but includes specific reference to the motivations of followers. In particular, path–goal theory places emphasis on the type of situation – and this includes both the task(s) and the skills and engagement of followers. Tasks can range from clear to quite opaque, and followers' skills and motivations can range similarly. Based on these variations, as illustrated in Figure 2.3, different leadership behaviours are required.

The three models (Theory X and Theory Y, the managerial grid, and path–goal theory) are illustrated below. They are included to exemplify the recurrent ideas in many of the theoretical developments of the time: they apply the basic principle from earlier behaviour theories that leadership behaviour and style are informed by being either task- or person-oriented and refer to appropriate behaviours to 'fit' the circumstances.

Two Types of Leader (Manager)	
Theory X Type	**Theory Y Type**
Believes	Believes
Followers not engaged	Followers are motivated and engaged
Need supervision	
Need incentivisation and penalties to manage performance	Do not need close management or scrutiny
Style is directive and controlling	Style is collaborative and supportive

Figure 2.1 McGregor's X Y Theory

Source: Adapted from McGregor (1960).

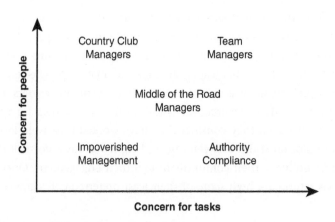

Concern for tasks

Figure 2.2 Blake and Mouton's managerial grid

Source: Adapted from Blake and Mouton (1964).

	HOW	USEFUL WHEN	
Directive	use of rules and authority	specifics are not clear in tasks and there is a need for close monitoring	Appropriate leader style is contingent on:
Supportive	supporting and encouraging followers	task is reasonably clear and followers can 'get on with it' but may need motivating	• follower characteristics (level of engagement and skills)
Participative	encourages follower autonomy and control	problem-solving required where follower ideas might be valuable.	• task characteristics
Achievement-oriented	followers are autonomous	task is opaque (e.g., new products) or other myriad outcomes are possible	

Figure 2.3 Path–goal theory

Source: Adapted from House (1971).

While the examples illustrated above are by no means a definitive set of context-informed behavioural leadership theories, they do illustrate the recurring themes of 'fit' between type of situation (most often task-based or person-based) and appropriate behaviour. The two theories that are outlined in more detail below are elaborated because they mark significant developments in our approaches to understanding leadership. Again, other theories were developed during this time, but each of the theories that follow represent seminal changes to how leading is understood and inspected. The first of these influential theories is contingency theory.

Contingency theory

First developed by the psychologist Fred Fiedler in 1967, contingency theory is based on the idea that leaders will be more or less suitable depending on the situation. Like other context-behaviour theories at the time, it proposes that some leaders are best for task-based situations, while other leaders are most suitable for people-centred leadership. The means by which Fielder was able to determine most suitable leadership matches was by using his least preferred co-worker (LPC) test. In this test, leaders are asked to identify the co-worker with whom they consider they have worked least well. From there, leaders are asked to plot on scales between one and eight various aspects of that co-worker, such as their friendliness, their commitment and their engagement. Once averaged, the leader who has returned a high score of their least preferred colleague is identified as a person-based leader, while the leader who has returned a low score is a task-based leader. The rationale for the distinction between person-based and task-based leaders is that a leader who returns a relatively positive LPC score is more tolerant and social than the leader who returns a score that suggests less sympathetic engagement with other people. As a consequence, the person-based leader is assumed to be more relationship-oriented and socially aware and the task-based leader less so. In addition, Fiedler finds via testing the LPC–leadership relationship in a number of settings, such as sports teams, military teams and commercial organisations, that for high LPC scorers, or person-based leaders, the most 'favourable' conditions are when their control and influence are moderate (e.g. a team leader). Conversely, for low LPC scorers, or task-based leaders, the most favourable conditions are when their influence and control are either high (e.g. a CEO or line manager) or when they are relatively low (e.g. a project manager). As this suggests, the model is complex, but as Fiedler notes in his 1995 paper where he reflects on his career as a theorist, the underpinning LPC measure has been tested and validated many times. The ensuing contingency theory that asserts that leaders should be matched appropriately to situations proposes further that leaders who are mismatched will experience stress and this will in turn affect performance.

Of course, our understanding of leadership has since evolved, but contingency theory and its underpinning psychological measures represent a clear line beyond which knowledge about leadership started to evolve. It included context and relationships with others as central factors in leadership, rather than the pure individualism of previous theorising.

At its simplest: Contingency theory, using LPC measures, proposes that optimal leadership is contingent on favourable conditions in a context requiring *either* a task-based *or* person-based leader.

Critique of contingency theory

In his own reflections, Fiedler himself critiqued his LPC and contingency theories (Fiedler, 1995). Along with other commentators of his time, he noted that it relied too heavily on the assumption that leadership is traits-based. Indeed, this is the central criticism of contingency theory: it assumes that a leader is one thing or another – is person-based or task-based – and therefore that a person should be deployed accordingly. This presumed lack of personal flexibility seems in current times to be a key error, but it was based on the principle that an individual's psychology is quite fixed – resonating again with older ideas about the orientations and actions of people being based on their traits or personality characteristics rather than in response to environment and circumstances. Nowadays, there is much clearer understanding that external influences can and do act to modify behaviours even if a person's psychology is relatively fixed and unalterable. Consequently, the behaviours of a person do vary according to context. As social beings, humans do act differently depending on the circumstances at hand and who they are with – a very clear and basic example is the difference between how people interact with others when they are at home compared to how they may act at work. Contingency theory does not account for this. Consequently, more social-informed theories of leadership began to emerge, where the focus moved beyond the individual and his or her specific psychology to allow that leadership occurs in social contexts, and, critically, is relational with followers. The following section outlines one of the most commonly referenced context-based theories, situational leadership theory, which builds on the idea that leadership is contingent on situation.

Situational leadership theory

One of the several theories to emerge after contingency theory was situational leadership theory (SLT). This was developed by Paul Hersey and Ken Blanchard, both scholars and practitioners in the business studies field. First presented in a paper in 1969 (where it was originally called 'life cycle theory'), SLT has been developed over the years, and not always consistently between the two original authors, though there was a mutually authored update in 1977. The consistent key premise of SLT is that leadership should be an appropriate fit to context. As in other theories, the situational leadership model identifies leadership as either task-based or person-based. In a departure from contingency theory, though, it allows that a leader may alter their approach according to circumstances and that a leader has the ability to be either task-oriented or person-oriented as appropriate depending on the situation. It is also one of the first theories that includes followers as a key part of considerations. Specifically, SLT proposes that there are four styles of leadership behaviour and that these should be deployed in response to what they call the 'readiness' of employees.

The four leading styles (S) are:

S1: directing (a clear instructional approach, often task-based)

S2: coaching (both instructional and supportive in order to achieve task completion)

S3: supporting (less instructional, encouraging followers to complete tasks using their own skills)

S4: delegating (leader is only peripherally involved in the task as it is delegated to the follower)

The four follower (development – D) types are:

D1: low ability and high motivation or willingness (e.g. people who are new and enthusiastic)

D2: some ability and lower motivation (e.g. skills are developed but enthusiasm has waned)

D3: moderate ability and no motivation (e.g. people are competent but lack challenge or interest in their job)

D4: high ability and high motivation (e.g. highly skilled and enthusiastic people)

For optimal performance amongst subordinates, leaders should determine the motivations and orientations of followers and adjust their style accordingly. This is modelled in Figure 2.4 below. Of note, rather than imply fixed and discrete categories, Figure 2.4 illustrates that within each general quadrant there are varying degrees to which leadership behaviour may be applied, and blurry lines between types.

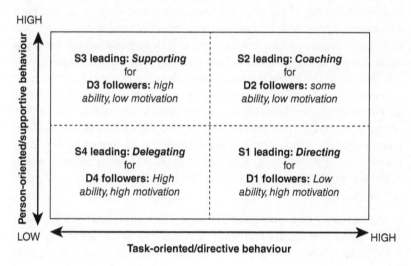

Figure 2.4   Situational leadership model
Source: Adapted from Hersey and Blanchard (1977).

As for contingency theory, SLT implies that leaders consider the context they are in. This consideration extends not just to the situation itself, though, as it includes too the people the leader is working with. SLT further provides, via the model, a more sophisticated framework from which leaders may make assessments about the readiness of followers and the context.

In a 1982 paper Hersey and Blanchard provided a very good example of how useful SLT can be for practitioners by describing how leaders of fire departments might change their behaviours in different circumstances. They note that when dealing with a fire, during the crisis or emergency task, a directive (perhaps even autocratic) style is required. In other circumstances, though, perhaps other styles are more appropriate. Hersey and Blanchard give the examples 'maintaining the equipment or studying new firefighting techniques', and recommend more person-based, supportive or even delegative approaches.

PERSPECTIVES FROM PRACTICE 2.1

John Black is a station manager with one of the UK's fire and rescue services. More information about John can be found on page 2.

John Black explains the contemporary situation in the UK fire and rescue context:

> A firefighter's day involves equipment maintenance, fire safety in the community and legislative work, intensive training on specialised equipment and training on the run of the mill bits of equipment that need to be practised with because none of the equipment is particularly easy to deal with: if you don't use it much you lose that skill very quickly and skill fade is a very big subject within the fire service. ... That's the way that the fire service is now run, that we will be skilled in a lot of areas and the skills are expected to be high in all areas. Also firefighters do home fire safety visits where fire crews go round and fit smoke detectors and give home fire safety advice. And all that is embedded into the normal day ... So there's non-emergency and emergency type of leadership needed. You have to change from a more consultative approach to a more urgent decision-making process. And it is literally that. It is moving from 'we will make decisions' to 'I will make decisions'.
>
> In an emergency you can divide an incident into stages: you have the emergency stage, the stabilisation stage and then the decay stage. And very much as an officer in charge, you cut up into these. In the emergency phase it is very clear to everybody exactly what they have to do, so it's easier to bark out instructions and ask people to do stuff and people will do stuff. If anyone doesn't obey – though this really never happens – they would be ordered to do it. If they wanted to give an opinion or challenge, it just wouldn't be listened to. It really never happens in the emergency phase of an incident. Because of the nature of the beast, because it is dangerous in every aspect, it's important that there's a very clear command and control structure that everybody understands. We always live by the idea that you do what you're asked to do and ask questions and criticise later if necessary. That's become a very formalised debrief nowadays, but we always used to have informal debriefs sitting round a canteen table drinking cups of tea and talking about things.

One of the most interesting aspects of looking into fires is that most of the injuries to firefighters are caused after the initial phase of the incident is under control, because everybody relaxes. Once we've got the initial rescues done, fire under control or vehicles under control, whatever it is, everybody relaxes and that's when injuries are more likely to occur. So throughout the incident, once the initial aims of the event are realised, it is important to create more aims, maybe not quite as urgent, but certainly aims that people know about in order that we decrease the amount of firefighter injuries. It is quite interesting to think about that. During a rescue there are very few injuries to firefighters. However, when we are cleaning up the mess that's when all the injuries occur.

Perspectives from practice questions

1. Why does John advocate a different leadership approach for emergency- and non-emergency-based work?
2. What type of leadership do you think is appropriate for:
    a. community safety work?
    b. routine training?
    c. phase 1 of an emergency incident?
    d. phase 2 of an emergency incident?

At its simplest: Situational leadership theory proposes that a leader may adapt his or her behaviour to best fit the situation and the orientation of followers.

Critique of situational leadership theory

The main criticism of SLT is that it categorises people, and wherever people or their behaviours are put into categories there will always be exceptions and outliers. Frankly, humans and their behaviours are not easily catalogued but the model does suggest people fit into discrete types (with admittedly blurry boundaries). Related to this, SLT suggests that leaders will find themselves dealing with similar follower types in a given situation. In many modern organisations this would just not be the case since a variety of personnel often work together on tasks or in groups. Indeed, over time the same individual follower may develop in terms of his or her skills and abilities and motivation. Consequently, SLT has been criticised for lacking long-term utility for practitioners. A further criticism is that, similar to other theories of the time, it reserves focus on the behaviours of leaders only, with leaders still assumed to be distinct from the group (see Chapter 4 for more on this).

As identified already, though, SLT evolved over some years and the authors have refined their model several times. Despite its limitations, it is one of the theories that marked a departure from considering a leader's personality or behaviours in isolation, and provided a framework that enhanced understanding of leadership in organisations, and from which flexible leadership practice in contexts and including consideration of followers could be informed.

PERSPECTIVES FROM PRACTICE 2.2

Victor Ikande is a regional head for the US-based construction firm Hollins. More information about Victor can be found on page 3.

Priyanka Thali is a managing editor at CACTUS Communications, a technology company headquartered in India. More information about Priyanka can be found on page 3.

Ken Lorenz is the owner of a data analytics firm and a data analytics consultancy, both based in the USA. More information about Ken can be found on page 2.

The leaders profiled throughout this book all referred to different types of leadership being appropriate for different followers and for different circumstances. For example, Victor Ikande notes of the building project portfolio he leads that some of the project teams require more input than others and this is determined by their complexity and scale:

> Some of my projects I only lead indirectly as oversight and they have their own project managers. So I'm not going to get myself involved in the day-to-day work, but we are a team and they'll deliver their project. So it's an oversight responsibility for those. You have to make sure they are all doing OK. But these are very senior people so, generally speaking, you don't need to hold their hands that much, if you know what I mean. They can deliver on their own. I just make sure there's an oversight watch on it. There are also some larger projects within the portfolio where I am there permanently as what we call the project executive or the project manager depending on what it is. On others again – the ones that are very big and complicated with different teams coming in and out – I'm running them full-time as the project manager.

Priyanka Thali refers directly to her tendency to alter her style depending on the circumstances of her managing editor role:

> I think what I learned over a period of time is that you can't stick to one style. It has to be a mix of styles depending on the situation at hand, as well as the people that you are working with. Not everybody responds well to one particular style and you have to kind of adapt your leadership styles. I think my natural leadership style would be a little more directive and based on compliance, but I think over a period of time I have been able to adapt that. I've been

forced to sometimes adapt how I manage a particular situation or a particular person, just based on what I think the situation requires, or how that person would respond best to it ... I have a mix of people on my team. I have the self-starters and then I have other people who are very dependent on somebody to direct them on what to do and I've had to adapt my style to get them to do what I need them to do.

Priyanka also notes the difference in terms of type of worker at CACTUS Communications:

With direct reports, because they are in-house employees, you can develop a relationship, not just because of the time factor or feasibility, but also con-tractually speaking. But when it comes to contractual [external] workers, there are certain limitations in terms of how much interaction or what kind of communication we can have with them. We do aim to try and make things as inclusive as possible ... And it depends again on what they need. I've seen that some contractual workers are fine just working on their own. They don't really need that kind of human touch. Whereas with some of the others they really like the fact that we speak to them on a regular basis.

Ken Lorenz reports similar to Priyanka in that he too notes that his approach to leading can depend on who he is working with:

I think it changes in every organization you're in. ... You can find types of peo-ple that will want to work the same way in the right job. I had people that had worked for me that had been in the same office for 20 years and had done a similar job for 20 years and they were great. They like to come into work, they're OK with the pay, and they did a great job and they never wanted to do anything more. They never wanted a promotion. They just were happy at that level. And then you have people who are driven by doing things the right way and some people who are driven by doing things the wrong way and some of them you're not gonna change.

John Black notes similar of the different personnel in a fire station:

It varies depending on the staff. Firefighters are different from other staff because they are there for different reasons. Firefighters can be easily moti-vated because they know there is promotion, and they are promotion-bound. But there are others who know that promotion just isn't there for them at all. For these other staff there are other encouragements you can do. For example, cleaning staff – hygiene is very important in a fire station because you have so many people sharing beds, sharing equipment, sharing towels,

(Continued)

washing facilities – so hygiene is very important. So it is important that the cleaning staff know that they are valued and you have to encourage them. But you can't encourage them through bonus schemes or money or promotion because these just aren't available for them. So your only option is to find alternative ways of rewarding them, by letting them leave early if they were finished their work, or even by remembering to say thank you.

Perspectives from practice questions

1. Why do you think Victor varies the level of input he has in different projects in his portfolio?
2. Why do you think Victor feels comfortable with laissez-faire leadership in some of his projects?
3. Why do you think Priyanka takes a different approach to different staff?
4. Is it appropriate to treat in-house and external contracted staff differently, as Priyanka suggests?
5. Ken suggests that some people are engaged and driven, some people are content but not ambitious, and some people are disengaged, even cynical about their workplace. What differences, if any, would you make to your leadership approach for each?
6. Why does the way John leads vary between firefighters and other types of staff?

SUMMARY: TRAITS AND BEHAVIOURS

In this chapter, the core principles of trait- and behaviour-based approaches to understanding how leaders conduct themselves are outlined. These signify the first steps amongst scholars to understand and analyse how leadership happens. Trait theory proposes that leading is somehow innate; it is an expression of a combination of elements of a personality. Critique amongst scholars exposes this understanding as limited for a variety of reasons, yet as we will explore in the next chapter, modern and present-day understanding of leadership shows clearly that the personality of a leader can be helpful (or alternatively, a hindrance) to their ability to lead.

From these early explorations of the traits of leaders, knowledge developed and began to appreciate that leadership is less about innate traits and more about behaviours. Circumstances also began to emerge as critical in considerations about how to lead, and particular distinction was made in several theories between leadership that was oriented towards having people engage in and complete tasks, and leadership that was oriented towards developing people to make contributions more generally in organisations. Several theories of the time make distinctions between different types of leader behaviour, from directive approaches most suited to tasks, through supportive and collaborative approaches, to laissez-faire approaches that afford staff autonomy (within organisational structures) over their own work and contributions.

As knowledge has evolved, so too has consideration of the spectrum of influences on leading in practice. While trait theory and early behaviour theories focus exclusively on the individual, later behaviour-based theories started to broaden the scope of analysis to include the contexts (most often using the task/person distinction). From there, followers were considered, and especially the extent of their skills and the levels of their engagement. The ensuing modern theories of leadership now account for leaders and followers, and critically the relationship between them. These are also central to analysis and development of understanding of how leadership happens and how organisations might optimise their approaches to leading in practice. The next chapter explores modern knowledge about leadership and particularly the much-studied and validated *Full Range of Leadership Model*.

EXERCISES

What are the main principles of trait theory?

Are traits important amongst leaders in modern organisations?

    Should leaders have specific traits?

    If so, which traits do you think are important for leaders in today's organisations?

Consider your own personality and traits:

    Which traits do you think you have that might support your ability to lead?

    Which do you think you lack?

What are the limitations of trait theory?

Explain the difference between task- and person-based leadership.

What are the main principles of behaviour-based theories?

Give an explanation of Theory X and Theory Y and path–goal theory.

Outline the principles of contingency theory.

Outline the principles of situational leadership theory.

How useful do you think behaviour-based theories are to leading in modern organisations?

Reflect on a leader with whom you are familiar. What is his or her behavioural approach?

3

MODERN APPROACHES TO LEADERSHIP

INTRODUCTION

Present-day knowledge and practice about leadership are informed by research from previous generations (as outlined in Chapter 2). This chapter moves on from traits, early behaviour theories and models of behaviours in contexts to explore a key part of the development of modern theory and practice of leadership. In this chapter, the core theoretical construct the *Full Range of Leadership* is explored.

Following on from behaviour- and situation-based approaches to understanding leading, leadership specialists began to appreciate that the way people are treated in context has a significant effect on their motivation and performance. As such, direct links between leadership and motivations theories gained credence. In particular, the idea (as discussed in Chapter 1 of this book) that motivations may be intrinsic or extrinsic informed how leading may be directed and optimised. This informed a rich seam of research and practice, including the ongoing development of the Full Range of Leadership Model (FRLM). In fact, this is not one theory, but several, each with its unique roots and developments. The collation of them to cover the spectrum of leadership used and developed in modern organisations is the combined work of many theorists and practitioners over the last 50 years, and a few of the most influential are included in the narrative that follows.

The FRLM is essentially a multi-factor model made up of three overlapping approaches to leading: *laissez-faire leadership* (or no leadership), *transactional leadership* and *transformational leadership*. In this chapter we will explore these component parts. In practice, the three core approaches to understanding how to lead inform each other; they are not discrete – in real organisational life elements of all are used. They are also the underpinning of many popular approaches to practising and developing leadership in organisations, such as authentic leadership, servant leadership and charismatic leadership. Each of these will be discussed towards the end of this chapter too.

THE FULL RANGE OF LEADERSHIP

In his 1985 book on leadership, the leadership and organisation studies scholar Bernard Bass introduced a multi-factor leadership questionnaire, which was variously refined (particularly with Bruce Avolio in 1990, and by Alimo-Metcalfe and Alban-Metcalfe in 2001). These questionnaires are designed to gauge an individual's approach to leading. These have been used and validated by many researchers over the years, and to this day they are still used to measure leader effectiveness in practice in organisations (e.g. Bass, 1998; Tracey and Hinkin, 1998; Antonakis et al., 2003). The multi-factor measurement underpins the Full Range of Leadership Model (Avolio, 1999; Avolio and Bass, 2002).

The FRLM includes *no leadership* and leadership on a *transactional–transformational* leadership continuum. In practice, most leading in organisations encompasses these general conceptualisations. Summary explanations of each are as follows:

- *Laissez-faire leadership* may be understood as no leadership, where leaders do not interfere with the activities of those they are managing.
- *Transactional leadership* may be understood as that which relies on a transaction between leader and follower – where followers perform in exchange for something.
- *Transformational leadership* may be understood as involving the development and support of followers so that they perform in order to fulfil ambitions that are aligned with those of the leader and the organisation.

Laissez-faire leadership, transactional leadership and transformational leadership emerged separately throughout studies of organisations and power (the principles of laissez-faire leadership, for example, were already well established throughout behavioural theories, as noted in Chapter 2). These ideas converge in the FRLM, though. Before exploring how they work together, the next few sections explore each broad concept in greater detail.

Transactional leadership

The ideas that underpin transactional leadership are not new; their origins are observable in the nineteenth-century works of Max Weber, the German economic and political sociologist (Weber, 1930). Weber proposed three types of authority: traditional (coercive) authority, legal (rational) authority and charismatic authority (heroism). Amongst his analyses of (Western) philosophical and economic life, Weber referred to *bureaucracy*, which he described as the rational-legal allocation of power and resources that make possible the development of a capitalist economic system. Within capitalism, effort is required of people throughout hierarchies, including the majority who do not own capital and have no ownership or direct interest in the outputs of the organisations they work in. Thus, Weber referred to the structures of society enabling power and systems that make work effort possible: via organisations, a worker exchanges effort within a social and legal structure for rewards required for survival in and membership of this socio-legal environment. In the 1970s, James McGregor Burns took these ideas and developed them for applicability in modern leadership practice, referred to since then as transactional leadership (Burns, 1978).

The transactional leader relies on bureaucratic control and authority that centres on rewarding and punishing followers to extract effort. In research published since Burns coined the term, there have been various developments to the idea of transactional leadership. Pertinently, the two key ideas of *contingent rewards* and *management by exception* have been extrapolated. *Contingent reward*, as outlined in Bernard Bass's book on leadership in the 1980s, refers to rewards that are contingent on good performance (Bass, 1985). This may involve timely and appropriate rewards that maintain motivation, or it may be completion-based – reward in exchange for a job well done. *Management by exception* is referred to as interference in the form of correction or punishment which may be either active (i.e. a leader monitors work to identify errors) or passive (i.e. a leader becomes involved only when things go wrong). In either case, unlike the management by exception referred to in Chapter 2 of this book, which implies trust and autonomy-affordance based on the idea that leaders become involved only when required, here management by exception, when discussed in the context of transactional leadership, is often associated with punishment in exchange for poor performance. Whether involving *management by exception* or *contingent reward* or both, transactional leadership relies on the idea that followers are not self-motivated, and instead perform in order to receive reward or avoid punishment.

The simple transactional nature of transactional leadership as a model is often linked to notions of 'getting things done', and as such is often discussed as ideal for *task-based* situations involving extrinsic rewards. Certainly, there is a mercenary quality to the idea of transacting for work effort, but in fact there is more to transactional leadership than that. Yes, it is true that in reality in organisations there is almost always transactional leadership at play, since in the modern commercial world people undertake work for income. This is a classic exchange of effort or labour for (extrinsic) financial reward. But transactional leadership is more complex than implying only extrinsic transaction orientation. While extrinsic drivers such as pay and other types of external reward are clearly transactional, so too are other drivers of behaviour, such as the opportunity to do work one enjoys, finds challenging or meaningful, or in some way enhances reputation or esteem. All of these may be described largely as intrinsic returns. So it is not a straightforward relationship between extrinsic motivation and transactional leadership – instead, it's important to understand the blurring of lines between all of these concepts and the overlapping nature of them.

In summary, transactional leadership involves:

- contingent reward; and
- management by exception, which may be either active (implying monitoring) or passive (implying intervention only when required).

At its simplest: Transactional leadership refers to leading in such a way as to enable transaction of effort for reward.

Transformational leadership

Transformational leadership refers to the development of the person, and as such it is often associated with *person-based* approaches to leading and intrinsic motivations. At the end of the last century, there was a substantial shift in research to focus on transformational theorising and techniques, and central amongst them were James McGregor Burns and Bernard Bass, but the theory was refined with input from others too, such as the leadership scholars Bruce Avolio and John Antonakis (see Burns, 1978; Bass, 1985; Antonakis et al., 2003).

The theory and practice of transformational leadership continue to evolve to this day, and so, as with all human developments, it is not a static construct, but instead may be understood as a set of techniques whereby a leader influences followers to extract effort. In particular, in Bass (1985) and Bass and Avolio (1990) two key elements of transformational leadership are described. These are:

a. transformational leadership involves both leaders and followers going beyond their immediate self-interests; and
b. transformational leadership links the interests of followers to those of leaders and organisations.

Transformational leadership thus involves a perspective that is wider than just getting the job done. It involves *developing people* and, critically, linking that development with organisational goals by aligning the interests of followers with the interests of the organisation they work in. To achieve this, trust is central to transformational leadership, as are respect, knowledge of and interest in followers, and the ability to provide opportunities for development of them.

These properties of transformational leadership have been grouped and modelled into four key parts that have become known as 'the four I's'. These are *idealised influence, inspirational motivation, intellectual stimulation* and *individual consideration*. A simple way of understanding these is to separate them into two sets: while each refers to approaches a leader might take, the first set has the leader as the focus, and the second has the followers. Box 3.1 illustrates:

Box 3.1: The four I's of transformational leadership

The leader

Idealised influence	The leader is an idealised version of the behaviours he or she seeks in followers. The leader is admired and respected. The leader is a role model who others want to emulate. *In short: the leader is charismatic.*
Inspirational motivation	The leader inspires people by communicating aims, ideas and tasks well. The leader is part of the team and is able to play their part. The leader communicates and acts with enthusiasm and motivates people by this behaviour. *In short: the leader inspires by communicating clearly and enthusiastically.*

The followers

Intellectual stimulation	The leader provides opportunities for followers to experience new roles and activities. Followers are given the opportunity to do things they enjoy and find fulfilling and are challenged and enabled to develop their skills and experiences such that they may rise in organisations. *In short: the leader develops and challenges followers.*
Individual consideration	The leader knows or at least acknowledges people as individuals with their own sets of skills, experiences and ambitions. Work and opportunities are linked to this knowledge. Followers are treated with their unique aims within the organisation in mind, rather than as collective and indistinguishable resources for deployment. *In short: the leader knows followers.*

A central element associated with transformational leadership is that it requires and engenders *trust*. Each of the pillars of leadership plays a part in this. In effect, followers must trust that a leader's idealised image is for real. They also must trust in the vision communicated by a leader and believe that their efforts will bring about the desirous outcomes. Trust is also required if people are to take on challenges and develop – a no-blame culture is required and they must trust the leader will support them. And finally, trust is central to the relationship required for individual consideration – to know and be known is relational.

In summary, transformational leadership involves:

- idealised influence;
- inspirational motivation;
- intellectual stimulation; and
- individual consideration.

At its simplest: Transformational leadership inspires and develops people, and performance is motivated by trust and aligning the goals of followers and organisations.

THE FULL RANGE OF LEADERSHIP MODEL

As explored in Chapter 1, extrinsic motivation relates to that which is external to a person – reward, punishment avoidance, etc. Alternatively, intrinsic motivation relates to that which is internal to a person – satisfaction, challenge, esteem, etc. As such, transactional leadership has often been associated with extrinsic motivations, and transformational with intrinsic ones. Similarly, transactional leadership has often been associated with *tasks and task completion*, while transformational leadership has been associated with *person-based* development. As noted, though, in practice it is more complex than that, since intrinsic rewards can be just as transactional as extrinsic ones, and extrinsic rewards are rarely received in a discrete, isolated way – consider the intrinsic rewards of pride and esteem if one is awarded an (extrinsic) increase in pay or bonus for good performance. So just as there are no clear lines between motivations or types of situation, neither are there clear lines when leading in practice. The FRLM allows for this blurring and overlap, and, in particular, transactional and transformational leadership have been described as poles on a continuum (Avolio, 1999), as shown in Figure 3.1.

As the continuum suggests, in practice leadership happens somewhere between transactional and transformational, and that will vary depending on the organisation, the leader, the followers, the circumstances, the task at hand, and any number of other variables. What is constant, though, is that no organisation in commercial or public life is entirely transactional, and equally, no organisation is entirely transformational. Instead, leadership approaches in organisations will be underpinned by both transactions and concern for people. In some cases, there will even be laissez-faire leadership (see Chapter 2 for

Figure 3.1 The transactional–transformational continuum

some examples of this). It is only the extent to which these approaches to leading are practised that varies from one organisation to another. In organisations that seek to develop people and extract best effort in the form of knowledge and creativity, a greater degree of transformational leadership may be appropriate. Transactions are still occurring, though – people will work for income and indeed, some of the development of a person itself may be transactional in nature (consider the opportunity to learn a new skill – it may be intrinsically rewarding and developmental, but also contingent-reward based). Equally, some work that appears entirely transactional in nature would nevertheless be soulless without some transformational leadership (consider the lowest skilled employee – intrinsic rewards such as pride and job satisfaction are still relevant drivers and retainers).

So it is critical to understand that, in practice, transactional leadership and transformational leadership are not discrete and in fact in organisations cannot really be separated from each other. When people work for organisations, yes they seek extrinsic reward, but engagement and ongoing contribution and commitment will be developed by transformational approaches that speak to a person's feelings of well-being, esteem and need to develop. Equally, though, while an organisation may spend much time developing the person and making sure the work is engaging and challenging and even enjoyable, if the developed person is not recognised by some extrinsic signal – such as pay or bonus or promotion – there is the risk of disengagement and demotivation. Further, there are no clear lines between what is transactional and what is transformational – challenge is intrinsically rewarding, for example, but the opportunity to conduct challenging work may well be transactional and linked to both the intrinsic reward and the addition of experience or skills to a résumé for transacting with in future. Chapter 5 explores some examples of how different approaches to leading may be implemented in practice in various contexts. For now, though, the FRLM is presented in Figure 3.2 to summarise the overarching concept.

Laissez-faire leadership
- No leadership

Transactional leadership
- Management by exception (active and passive)
- Contingent rewards

Transformational leadership
- Idealised influence (charisma)
- Inspirational motivation
- Intellectual stimulation
- Individual consideration

Figure 3.2   The Full Range of Leadership

Critique of the FRLM and transactional–transformational approaches to understanding leadership

As noted, transactional–transformational leadership is underpinned by the multi-factor leadership scales, and this is one of the key areas of critique. There are now several versions of the multi-factor questionnaire, with differing amounts of questions. All of these are scale questions where respondents score themselves as 'least to most likely' to exhibit behaviours (Bass and Avolio, 1990). Underpinned by an instrument of this type, the criticism can always be levied that responses will depend entirely on a person's self-reflection. The extent to which people are able to make accurate assessments of their own actions and behaviours will vary, and it is possible that even the same person could answer differently on different days. That said, the questionnaire has been applied by researchers in all sorts of contexts and all over the world, as have the component theories of transactional and transformational leadership. Prabhakar (2005), for example, presents an international study across 28 countries of the effectiveness of transformational leadership techniques in projects (a topic we will pick up on again in Chapter 5). The transactional–transformational leadership concept thus remains a useful tool for understanding behaviour and reflecting on leadership styles, strengths and weaknesses.

The other key criticism of the transactional–transformational continuum understanding of leadership is that it maintains the idea that leading involves the leader as the only key focus. While the whole continuum refers to motivations and followers, and transformational leadership in particular proposes means by which to influence and engage people, it does so from the exclusive viewpoint of developing the leader.

These limitations of course create the conditions whereby theoretical and practice refinements can be made. And that brings us right up to the present day in terms of understanding how knowledge and practice about leading have developed. The FRLM broadly has brought about the idea that leadership involves leaders *and* followers. The next step was to explore in more detail the relationship between them. Chapter 4 explores some of the most recent thinking on the relational and reciprocal properties of leadership, leading to new ways of thinking about it as emergent and distributed throughout organisations. The FRLM still resonates throughout knowledge and practice of leadership, though, especially in organisations, and it underpins much of the effort and provision made available in organisations to develop leadership, a topic we will return to in Chapter 9. For now, the following presents testimony that evidences some of the approaches our participant leaders take in their respective contemporary organisations.

PERSPECTIVES FROM PRACTICE 3.1

Priyanka Thali is a managing editor at CACTUS Communications, a technology company headquartered in India. More information about Priyanka can be found on page 3.

Jannie Tam is the founder of the Hong Kong-based talent development company GROWDynamics. More information about Jannie can be found on page 1.

John Black is a station manager with one of the UK's fire and rescue services. More information about John can be found on page 2.

Claire McCarthy is the Director of Operations and HR at a large children's charity in Wales. More information about Claire can be found on page 2.

Victor Ikande is a regional head for the US-based construction firm Hollins. More information about Victor can be found on page 3.

Ken Lorenz is the owner of a data analytics firm and a data analytics consultancy, both based in the USA. More information about Ken can be found on page 2.

Priyanka's approach in publishing

For Priyanka Thali in her role as managing editor at CACTUS Communications, her own conduct and actions are important. She states:

> Self-awareness is very important. As a leader it will help you understand yourself and it will also help you manage other people better because you will also gain an understanding of how others see you and you will be able to influence how other people see you if you are aware of yourself. This would be my main advice to anybody who's seeking to be a leader. And of course be open: be open to change and be open to learning and advice. Everything doesn't have to filter down from you, you can learn a lot from your team as well. Be open to ideas from your subordinates that might be better than yours. I think what has worked for me is being approachable. People know that they can come to me for anything and they see me as a human. I'm not this perfect person that can do no wrong. I do make mistakes and I'm not shy to cast light on those mistakes. If something does go wrong, I'll be like, 'OK, you know what, this was my bad'. And they see you as somebody who is capable of slipping up once in a while and who is not shy of owning it. I think it's just about leading by example. And them knowing that they can talk to me about anything. I've tried to make communication as open as possible, and I also try to foster that across team members. So we have team meetings on a regular basis where we discuss just about anything – updates, targets, stuff like that – so everybody is aware of what the others are doing. I think open communication is the key to it. I think that to maximise on your

team's potential you need to know them deep down. So it's about having more conversations with them. I speak to them almost on a daily basis on the phone or by text. And I have one-on-one discussions as frequently as I can. And what comes out of these conversations is you get to know what drives them, or what gets them down, what their interests are. And everybody needs an opportunity to learn and advance themselves. People need an equal platform and opportunities to advance, and that's why it's important to develop independent thinkers. A very important tool that I use is appreciation. In our line of work, and everywhere, slip-ups or negative feedback gets shared very quickly, but a lot of good work goes unnoticed. So I make a point of looking at stuff that went well and appreciate the responsible team member; it's important that they know they're doing well. We've gotten to a point where all of us trust each other. They trust my leadership, and of course, I trust them.

Jannie's approach in a small firm

Well, for me, I cannot be fake. I think as a leader you have to be authentic as well and people need to see how you persevere and how you press on. Also, I don't micromanage. You need to build this intrinsic trust, but at the same time you have to look at the shared vision. I mean you bring the big picture to everyone, but they also can chip in their ideas, so they own the big picture too. You have to make sure that everyone feels a sense of ownership in the bigger picture, so they will put in more of themselves and they also feel like they can flourish and feel proud of what they do. Many people feel like their only value is to do things that make their boss look good. I decided that I would take consequences – they [followers] take the credit and I take the consequences. And then we are able to have a pretty trusting relationship. I try to convey that I'm there to help them succeed.

John's approach in the fire service

I'm very consultative. You need as much information as you possibly can to influence your decisions. And your decisions would be made, based not only on your own opinions, but you take others' ideas into account. So, yeah, I solicit all sorts of opinions. I listen to their opinions and make an assessment. And my approach is 'Come and talk to me if you've got a problem'. I regularly meet with the crews and they always have an opportunity to either discuss a fire or the latest community initiative in an informal fashion. So we always speak, whether that be by getting the crews together to sit and discuss stuff that we think is important, or over a cup of tea or a cup of coffee. I just sit with the crews talking about just exactly what problems

(Continued)

there might be and issues of the day. So I am very consultative but it was understood that when we went to an incident I am in charge and all decisions are through me. But at the same time, as long as they do what I ask them to do and don't put themselves in danger, they can always come back and discuss it later. So there is always a feedback loop, always, even at an emergency. And if performance drops below requirements, you always have to make sure that your communications lines are open and you are diplomatic in your response.

Claire's approach in the charity sector

I try and bring people on board. Change in particular can worry people so I have to demonstrate that it will make life better, it will make life easier, and show people that if we do things this way it will be a bit quicker and a bit easier. It's not about going in with a full, 'Right I'm going to eradicate this system'. And I think people do get on board with you if you've got a little bit of patience and try to understand where they're coming from, what is it they're worried about. And I think if you are open to collaboration with people, they sense that, they get that from you, as opposed to, 'Well, I'm going to change it and that's the way it's going to be!'. And together you problem solve. Also, if you give people a little bit of responsibility and say, 'Right you're to take charge of this', people do care about it more. If you're sitting right now doing work that someone else is going to check later anyway, people don't care. Also, people like to be acknowledged. We use a workplace social media app, which is an online group for staff, and often what's on it is photographs of somebody who is proud of something they've done. That can be any department. So that then leads to their job being much more visible and that makes people feel valued, it makes them feel like they're not hidden away in a corner doing something that nobody knows about. And I've noticed that even people that profess to be quite shy and don't need that kind of attention, they actually do like it when they get that recognition.

Victor's approach in construction

Victor believes pay and reward are important but not the whole story. He explains his position thus:

Pay is not a standalone motivational technique, but it's definitely an extremely important one. It is not the only thing, right? But knowing that you're rewarded for the level of responsibility you have is absolutely critical. In fact, I genuinely see it as part of my job to get the best possible pay cheque I can get for you. If I feel someone is underpaid, I think it's part of my job to make sure that they are paid the right amount of money. I've been successful at retaining people that way, but there are two cases where we have experienced major losses of people because we didn't make the move quickly enough and they departed the organisation. These were two big strategic losses. And yes, those people went away because our competitors with the same project portfolio offered better pay. They are international companies so pay is important. But it's not the whole story. One of the things that I do is create that psychological safety. When people believe that they have that, quite often it makes you tap into the best part of their talent. If you ask me what is the single most powerful tool, it's that. When people are not worried about what you're thinking, when people don't think that you think negatively about them and they just feel safe around you, then they bring their real self to work and more often than not they bring their best self to work. If people feel heard, they feel they are not disconnected from you and it spreads. I make the next line of people, the next layer of leaders under me, feel that way and they perceive they are valued and it has this domino effect that's quite powerful because they mirror that leadership because they can clearly see the rewards of it. Once that framework is there right, it's inclusive and it's all part of the trust game. And when you make decisions, because you have built those relationships, people might not always agree with you, but they will go with your call.

Ken's approach as an entrepreneur

As noted in Chapter 1, Ken also believes extrinsic rewards are important, but as he puts it:

When you're not interested in the work, it doesn't matter what the pay and the perks are. You have to find what motivates people. I try to make sure people are doing things because they want to. The best advice I was ever given was 'trust but verify'. You can trust them to go off and build stuff, but make sure you verify that you're getting what you expected. You don't have to check everything and micromanage it, but there are points when you need to check. In business one of the best leaders I had was one who gave me this advice. He also he gave me the opportunity and the freedom to go try things like, 'Hey, I have this great idea', and he gave me the money and scope and, you know, some of them didn't work out, and some of them were huge successes, but he always let me go try it and prove it. So yes, I definitely let people contribute: 'How would you run this? What would you do differently to make this work? Alright, let's see if that's something we can do.' And you have to make sure people are comfortable raising a hand and saying 'we have problems, we have issues', and you have to make it a comfortable work environment. I've had too many times [in previous jobs] where it's, 'We don't want to tell him that things are broken or this isn't right'. I think the culture of no bad news happens

(Continued)

a lot. Everyone just wants to be positive, especially if you're very focused on revenue. And nobody wants to mention that the bottom is going to drop out or there's a problem. You can look at some companies now that are a shell of where they were and where profits have gone down. And you're like, 'Maybe this is not a place I want to be'. In a data company one thing we want is for it to be right. We're not concerned if you need to ask for help to get there. If I can see that there's some struggle, we can talk about your problem and try to come up with a solution. And I'm always here to bounce ideas off. I think it's hard for someone to come to you unless you make it easy. If people aren't comfortable with you or they don't know how to gauge your reaction to bad news they're gonna be less likely to give it.

Perspectives from practice questions

1. Outline any consistencies you observe between the approaches taken in the six testimonies.
2. The six leaders above each refer to a different commercial or industrial context. Can you see any differences in leadership approaches that are attributable to the different contexts?
3. What evidence for any of the four I's of transformational leadership can you see in the testimonies of the leaders?
4. With reference to any of the approaches presented above, explain the transactional and transformational elements of the approach and any overlaps between these.
5. Where on the transactional–transformational leadership continuum would you plot each of the six leaders profiled, based on the excerpts above?
6. Can you see any links between any of the approaches suggested by the testimonies and any of the theories of motivations in Chapter 1, or older or context-based theories of leadership behaviours in Chapter 2?

Extensions to and overlaps amongst modern approaches to leading

The development of theory and practice in any human behaviour is never linear. Leadership is no exception to this, and there has been much overlap and complementarity amongst theory and research as knowledge has developed. Some of the key overlaps in leadership scholarship relate to modern popular conceptualisations and practices of leading and there are several theoretical developments that are applied variously, and often depending on organisational context, that have transactional–transformational types of conceptualisations at their roots. Below we outline some of the types of leading most frequently discussed in contemporary popular, scholarly and organisational rhetoric: *charismatic leadership*, *authentic leadership* and *servant leadership*. Each is discussed in brief below.

Charismatic leadership

Around the same time Burns was writing what would become the underpinning ideas about transactional and transformational leadership in the 1970s, Robert House was applying another of Weber's principles of authority, *charisma*, to leadership. In House (1977) and later developed in Shamir et al. (1993) the theory of *charismatic leadership* is presented and explained (later critiqued by the business and leadership scholar Gary Yukl in a 1993 paper). Charismatic leadership relies on the ability of a leader to influence followers by sheer force of personality. It owes much to trait theory since charisma is defined as a set of innate features of a character. But it also refers to behaviours (see Chapter 2 for more on both trait- and behaviour-based approaches to understanding leadership). In Chapter 2, there is discussion about the limitations of trait theory for understanding leadership. Despite these limitations, there are examples of leaders throughout the world and throughout history who have influenced and affected behaviour and performance of others by being charismatic, and indeed most people have experience of charismatic leaders somewhere in their lives (the extent to which this is a force for good or not is explored in Chapter 8 on ethics).

From a knowledge development point of view, over the years, leadership theory and practice have seen convergence of the ideas underpinning transformational and charismatic leadership. In particular, along with many other researchers, Bruce Avolio and John Antonakis have written extensively on charismatic leadership (Howell and Avolio, 1992; Antonakis, 2012; Avolio and Yammarino, 2013).

It is possible to describe charismatic leadership as transformational leadership with a particular and amplified focus on idealised influence. It is also clear that charisma is a key element in relationships between leaders and followers.

Authentic leadership

Authentic leadership is another development in recent thinking about approaches to leading. Developed as a theoretical model by Avolio, and particularly with William Gardner (Gardner et al., 2005), authentic leadership has trust front and centre, and is resonant of leadership heavily influenced by a leader's values and belief in a cause or course of action. Authentic leadership may be described as leadership that is driven by a leader's commitment to change or improvement or service to a cause. Informed by the FRLM methodology, a multi-factor questionnaire that engages directly with the practice of authentic leadership is developed and presented in Walumbwa et al. (2008), and this has been used as a means by which to measure and test the practice of authentic leadership in organisations.

(Continued)

Authentic leadership is often associated with ethical leadership, though the links between acting ethically as a leader and acting authentically as a leader are inconclusive. Nevertheless, when we think about values-based leadership, leaders across the world and throughout history who have led from a moral high ground are often cited as authentic leaders (see Chapter 8 for more on this). For authentic leaders, it is the trust followers have in the sincerity of their commitment to a cause or objective that motivates.

It is possible to describe authentic leadership as transformational leadership with a particular and amplified focus on inspirational motivation.

Servant leadership

Servant leadership describes an approach to leading that puts the leader in the role of servant. In this sense, a servant leader's focus is to serve a community in some way, whether that community is made up of followers or clients or other beneficiaries of the work. From a leader–follower perspective, the leader serves the followers rather than the other way round.

Servant leadership was developed by Robert T. Greenleaf, a retired manager with a long career of working in leadership roles in the USA. Based on his experiences and expertise, he developed the servant leadership model and created the Greenleaf Center for Servant Leadership, a non-profit organization to advance knowledge and practice of servant leadership (www.greenleaf.org).

Servant leadership is based on nine key principles. These are:

- Listening
- Empathy
- Awareness
- Persuasion
- Conceptualisation
- Foresight
- Stewardship
- Growing people
- Building communities.

The rationale behind servant leadership is a move away from directive and authoritarian styles of leading, and instead focuses on developing people so that they can become the next generation of leaders, with a view to contribution and service that will enrich individuals and organisations. Again, this resonates with the principles in transformational leadership, with its focus on personal development and (service-based) relationships between leaders and followers.

It is possible to describe servant leadership as a type of transformational leadership with a key focus on inspirational motivation and individual consideration. It is also clear that the notion of service to followers is a fundamentally relational idea.

Some of the latest thinking on leading that departs from the traditional focus on the individual is explored in the next chapter. Before that, though, it is timely at this point to turn to the developing conceptualisation of followership – a critical element in the theory and practice of leadership.

FOLLOWERSHIP

Around the same time much of the seminal work on the FRLM was being developed, research was also inspecting the role of those being led – the followers – in organisations. In fact, the role of followership has been a topic of intellectual consideration throughout history and in all cultures across the world, but it was little considered in the development of knowledge about leadership until the researcher Robert Kelley published a seminal paper on it. Kelley (1988) presents a typology of followers, including the types *passive, alienated, conformist, exemplary* and *pragmatic*, as shown in Table 3.1.

Kelley's typology marked the start of a shift in thinking about leadership, since it acknowledged that the engagement of followers is as much a critical influence on leadership as leaders are on follower engagement. In Kelley's model, the most effective type of follower is *exemplary* since this describes followership that constructively engages participation and contributes criticality, knowledge and value-adding. As such, it is *exemplary* engagement that should be optimally cultivated by leadership. Refined typologies have been introduced since, including in Brown and Thornborrow in the 1990s and another from Potter and Rosenbach in 2006. Table 3.2 illustrates the basic types in each of these and they are included as examples of a field that continues to develop (in particular, Crossman and Crossman (2011) provide a good summary).

In Brown and Thornborrow (1996), it is *effective and exemplary* followership engagement that is optimal for organisations; in Potter and Rosenbach (2006) it is *partner*. Along with Kelley's original *exemplary* type, these examples of ideal follower engagement all describe active participation, independence and autonomy, and are suggestive of a relationship between leader and follower that has partnership qualities rather than subordinate ones (Kelley, 1988). This moves us towards understanding most effective leadership as involving the *relationship* between leaders and followers, and the emergence of a view

Table 3.1   Kelley (1988) follower types

passive	Passive and uncritical thinkers
alienated	Independent thinkers but passive and disgruntled
conformist	Competent and obedient but lack critical engagement and independence
exemplary	Independent thinkers able to engage critically and constructively
pragmatic	Compliant with the leader, expedient engagement

Table 3.2   Example followership models

Brown and Thornborrow (1996)		Potter and Rosenbach (2006)	
Effective and exemplary	Independent thinkers, enthusiastic, problem solvers	*Subordinates*	Lack initiative, not inclined to take responsibility
Survivors	Capable and adaptable but lack independence	*Politician*	Strategic and calculating in relationships
'Yes' people	Obedient and submissive	*Contributor*	Capable and contributory but lack independence
Sheep	Lack initiative, take little responsibility, passive	*Partner*	Independent participants, enthusiastic
Alienated	Independent but dissatisfied in the organisation		

of leadership as a process associated with *community* and involving the enablement of followers. These are both discussed later. For now, the key point of note is that throughout the literature there are tests of the relationship between leadership styles and follower effectiveness, and, regardless of followership model applied, across these researches the use of transformational approaches and the importance of relations between leaders and followers have been observed to enhance most effective followership (Dvir and Shamir, 2003, Uhl-Bien et al., 2014 and Alegbeleye and Kaufman, 2020 are just a few examples).

The focus on followership and engagement marks a significant part of the departure – in theory at least – from considering leadership as concerning individuals and their personalities and behaviours in isolation. Instead, current research and knowledge about leading tends to treat it as embedded in community in some way, where there is an ongoing and dynamic interchange between leaders and followers. This is discussed throughout the next chapter.

SUMMARY

Developed understanding of followership, along with the FRLM and an associated ongoing focus on the importance of transactional and transformational approaches, has served to inform the next steps in the evolution of the theory and practice of leadership. The newest ideas take the leader–follower relationship, and rather than focus on the leader and how he or she might influence followers, they focus on the relationships and groups within organisations and explore how leadership may develop to best meet the needs of work, life and business in the global present and future worlds. As such, the most recent theory and practice about leading is starting to depart from notions of leadership exclusively as the property of individuals. Instead, the focus of research and practice in some organisations is shifting to explore ways of developing leadership as a community or group practice and involving the relationships therein. These are discussed in the next chapter.

EXERCISES

What are the key principles of transactional and transformational leadership?

Explain the four I's of transformational leadership.

Can you name some famous authentic leaders, charismatic leaders, servant leaders, historical or contemporary (and you will find plenty of overlaps)? Explain your reasons for your categorisations.

Consider your current or previous workplace. Can you identify amongst your leaders there any examples of transactional or transformational leadership?

Consider your own approaches to any communal activity – do you think you are (or will become) a servant, authentic or charismatic leader?

Reflect on your own experience. What kind of follower have you been in different organisations? Did this vary?

What types of followers do you observe in your own organisation?

How would you develop followers to be actively engaged and participatory?

4
NEW TRENDS IN UNDERSTANDING LEADERSHIP

INTRODUCTION

The conceptual developments embodied in the Full Range of Leadership Model (FRLM) have been a springboard from which further theory and practice continue to evolve. The focus on the links between leaders and followers, in particular, has been a key milestone in understanding leadership, and the role of leadership on organisational performance remains a core topic. As knowledge about leadership, and about leading people in organisations in particular, has evolved, and as the practices, needs and expectations of leaders and followers have developed globally, by the turn of the millennium, theorists were beginning to explore ways of leading that would meet the needs of an increasingly complex and interconnected world. As such, what has emerged most recently is increased focus on leadership *throughout* organisations. In particular, following the evolution of leadership knowledge, there is greater understanding of and emphasis on the *relational* qualities of leading and the importance of people-centred approaches to it in both theory and practice. Leader–member exchange theory is a pertinent example of theory that puts the relational qualities of leading at front and centre. Emerging in the early years of the twenty-first century, it moves on from the FRLM and transformational leadership in particular, and marks a point from which theories about the emergence and distribution of leadership could develop. Some of these are discussed later in this chapter, but before we get to these, it is important to explain the leader–member exchange theory first.

LEADER–MEMBER EXCHANGE THEORY

Leader–member exchange theory (LMX) marks a departure from previous theorising about leading in one key way: it includes explicitly that leadership is relational. Where the FRLM has relationships as an implicit component by highlighting the person-centred properties of transformational techniques, LMX has as the core focus not the leaders nor the followers, but, critically, the relationship between them. Central to this is the idea that the better the relationships amongst people who are working together to achieve outcomes, the better the performance of those people and the quality of the outputs.

Developed by various people over the last three decades, but notably Mary Uhl-Bien and George Graen, LMX has at its heart the two-way relationship between leaders and followers, placing these relationships as central to effective leadership (Graen and Uhl-Bien, 1995). These relationships are explained as dyads (i.e. between two actors: leader and follower). As a dyad, the leader–follower relationship moves beyond the relationship of a leader with a set of followers, and instead is about the reciprocal relationship each follower has with a leader. Critical in organisational life is the fostering of good and productive dyads and these depend on the character and activities of both followers and leaders. These relationships form and develop over time and include various stages, from the 'vertical dyad' between leaders and followers, through to the creation of teams (or 'aggregate dyads') made up of intertwining relationships. Good rapport and trust within these relationships have been linked to high-quality outputs in terms of organisational performance.

At its simplest: LMX proposes that leading in organisations is relational, and leaders and followers develop dyads.

Critique of LMX

Embedded in LMX is the fact that not all relationships between leaders and followers will be equal and inevitably some followers will form better relationships with leaders than others, potentially leading to in-groups and out-groups. While in-groups may well be productive, this may also lead to demotivation for some and be divisive at an organisational level. Similarly, the clear links between the personality of a leader and his or her ability to develop rapport and trust amongst followers suggests that some dyads have the potential to be bad for performance since the focus is on the relationships rather than the effectiveness of the leadership process. It also risks the potential for manipulation or even exploitation of followers (a toxic kind of leadership) as followers strive to be in favour (see Chapter 8 for a discussion of the ethics of toxic relationships in organisations). In addition, while LMX positions leadership as relational, similar to all the theories that have preceded, it still treats the leader as an individual within a hierarchy. As such, from a research point of view, there is a suggestion of *headship* rather than actual leading, and the fundamental position of leadership as individualistic and exceptional prevails.

Despite these limitations, LMX, like the FRLM, are points from which theory and practice have developed right up to the present day. Most recent theory and knowledge development about leadership tends to involve a marked departure from the links between leadership and headship, to explore leading as relational, potentially emergent and distributed in organisations, and thus requires exploration that goes beyond inspection of the styles and behaviours of individuals. It is to this that we turn next.

BEYOND THE INDIVIDUAL

LMX theory marks a significant step towards knowledge and understanding leadership in the modern world. However, like previous theories and practices, LMX still positions leadership as the domain of an individual. More recent theorising about leadership is moving beyond that and looking at leading as a set of phenomena in organisations. Some of this new thinking resonates with the conceptual distinction between *leadership* and *headship*. As noted in Chapter 1, *headship* signals seniority in rank and role but does not necessarily imply any competence in leadership. Meanwhile, leadership, as defined as an ability to envision (*thought leadership*) or to influence others (*leading people*), may be observable throughout organisations, and not just in designated roles in the traditional hierarchy (see Chapter 5 for more on this). Elsewhere, there has been focus on making a distinction between *leading* as the property of an individual, and *leadership* as a feature of organisational culture. As discussed in this chapter in the section on *collective leadership*, the term '*leaderful*' has also been added to the analysis by Raelin (2021).

The organisational behaviour scholar Declan Fitzsimons explains that the modern world, with its inter-connectedness and dynamism, moves so fast that it is no longer reasonable to expect that an individual holds the capacity to be able to react to all circumstances, information, opportunities and threats. Instead, sharing or delegation or some other type of pluralism is a more appropriate means by which to inject a range of skills and experiences into leadership (Fitzsimons, 2016). This does not suggest a need for more leadership roles (in fact, often headship). Instead, it suggests a need to rethink what leadership is, what it is for and how it might best support organisational culture and goals. This moves research and practice of leading beyond the realm of the single authority-based leader.

Knowledge about and development of leadership beyond the individual are often described as *post-heroic leadership*. Indeed, the whole idea of leadership as somehow embodied within one person is increasingly regarded by scholars as limited. The inherent exceptionalism, in particular, is seen as stereotyping leadership so that lack of fit with the stereotype immediately disadvantages some people in terms of developing into leadership roles. In their book on identity and leadership, Ford et al. (2008) explain that leaders are most often discussed in terms that are masculine and suggest control, competitiveness and individualism (and we will discuss some of this stereotyping in Chapter 6 on diversity and leadership). Joanna Probert and Kim Turnbull James refer to the idea that we all have an *implicit leadership theory*. This comprises our ideas about what leadership is, what it looks like and how it is expressed, and this is learned and developed throughout our experiences. In organisations, these notions are collated and embedded as institutionalised norms and become the *leadership concept*. An organisation's *leadership concept* is the collective and formalised ideal of leadership in the specific organisational context. In many organisations, the *leadership concept* is charged with reproducing leadership styles and approaches that may have worked in the past, but may not work in the future (Probert and Turnbull James, 2011). We will return to *implicit leadership theory* and an organisation's *leadership concept* in Chapter 9 on leadership development and training, but for now they are summarised as shown in Box 4.1.

Box 4.1: Perceptions and leadership

Implicit leadership theory – describes our personal ideas about what a leader is, what a leader looks like, and how a leader acts. These perceptions of leadership are influenced by our experiences of leaders throughout our lives and take root in our expectations about what leadership is and what it should be.

The leadership concept – describes the crystallisation of implicit leadership theories into an organisation's expectations of what leadership is, what it looks like and how it is enacted. It is influenced by how leadership structures are organised and what leaders have done and looked like in the past. In organisational life, the leadership concept can lead to reproduction of a type of leader or approach to leadership. This consistency can benefit an organisation, but equally may disadvantage it over time as modes of working, expectations of followers and other stakeholders, and the commercial environment evolve to a stage where the organisation's *leadership concept* may become stale, out of date and inappropriate for ongoing success. The other potential problem with it is that if one does not 'fit' the concept for some reason, one may not be seen as having leadership potential, leading to disadvantage for diverse individuals, and potentially loss of talent and opportunity for the organisation. An organisation thus should critique its *leadership concept* in order to inspect its ongoing fit for purpose and value.

The personal and communal perceptions about leadership that make up our *implicit leadership theories* and the *leadership concept* in organisations are informed and underpinned by the idea that the leader is an individual with specific qualities, attitudes and approaches to work and to engaging followers. Therefore, despite so much advance in knowledge in terms of linking leaders and followers–taking account of contexts and motivations, philosophical position and values–ultimately in practice we often still associate leadership with a set of traits and behaviours exhibited by individuals, and it appears many organisations still rely on stereotypes or older archetypes of how leaders present and conduct themselves. In the complex, globally connected modern world, there is a rationale that the way we view and practise leading has to evolve. It is to this that we turn next.

LEADERSHIP AND PLURALISM

Pluralism describes conditions and situations where more than one authority is present. In pluralist societies, people of different backgrounds, social philosophies and faiths can co-exist allowing that they may or may not hold similar beliefs. In pluralist structures there is no single moral or philosophical authority, but instead an acceptance and tolerance of a range of opinions, ideas and values. These may complement or sit in opposition to each other but, critically, they co-exist and together form a new type of shared community. Leadership that is pluralist thus describes leadership that may derive from more than one source and involves an inclusive approach to the functions and practices of leading. This may include a blurring of the leader–follower distinction, to the point where they may not even be regarded as discrete from each other, and the social and organisational culture and strategy emanate from co-creation amongst a wide set of stakeholders. Thus, pluralism, when applied to leadership, suggests a perspective that takes it beyond the focus on the individual to a much more inclusive set of practices. In a 2012 review of the literature about pluralist approaches to leadership, Jean-Louis Denis and colleagues identify four main streams of research: *shared leadership, pooled leadership, distributed leadership* and *relational leadership* (Denis et al., 2012). More recently the concept of *collective leadership* has been added (Raelin, 2021). Each of these is outlined below.

Shared leadership

Shared leadership describes a situation whereby an appointed leader gives responsibility and authority to persons in his or her team who are not in leadership roles. The official leader thus delegates or creates an organisational culture where delegation can occur as optimal amongst a team. The purpose of this delegation is to match the most appropriate person in the team to the task, issue or challenge at hand, and so while the official leader may retain oversight of activities, it is the most qualified, experienced or otherwise most suitable person who will direct activity and effort for specific tasks or functions. In their book on shared leadership, Craig Pearce and Jay Conger describe how shared leadership is iterative in that it involves constant change and reciprocity in relationships.

Consequently, good relations and knowledge are important, including knowledge of lead-ers about followers and knowledge of followers about leaders and fellow followers. As such, in an organisation these relationships may be vertical and hierarchical or lateral across teams (Pearce and Conger, 2003).

Importantly, shared leadership is not necessarily systematic or formally structured. The leader remains the leader and delegation is informal (though not necessarily unrewarded). It requires the knowledge about people as individuals that comes from transformational leadership (specifically *individual consideration*) and is relational, so it is based on trust and respect for the skills and experiences of followers, resonating further with transforma-tional techniques and relational approaches to leadership.

At its simplest: Shared leadership occurs where a designated leader shares responsi-bilities and authority across a team as appropriate to their skills and experiences.

Pooled leadership

Pooled leadership describes the pooling of leaders so that no single individual is in over-all charge of a team or business unit. Pooled leadership therefore involves two or more people being appointed to and sharing a leadership role. This is a formal and structurally designated sharing of leadership and is based on an organisational aim of increasing the number and range of leaders in charge of specific parts of the organisation. The pooling of leaders is intended to allow for dialogue and knowledge exchange between leaders with potentially different but complementary skills and experiences, and it therefore also spreads the range of knowledge and expertise in the leadership unit. In practice, pooling leadership keeps the hierarchical structure in place, but broadens the range of information, skills and approaches to leading in teams. It thus requires good working relationships, mutual respect and trust amongst leaders.

At its simplest: Pooled leadership is the pooling of two or more people into a joint leadership role.

Distributed leadership

Distributed leadership comprises a clear departure from the traditional hierarchical struc-tures of leadership. Rather than leadership occurring in a top-down system, it is instead distributed throughout an organisation so that leadership may be conducted by people throughout teams and throughout organisational hierarchies. This is suggestive of a more matrixed approach to leadership that allocates responsibility throughout the organisa-tion rather than from the top-down orientations of traditional thinking and practice of leadership. There are many organisations where versions of distributed leadership are observable, where there are teams within larger units each with their own specialism and leadership. These may not be particularly high in organisational structure terms, but they are bestowed authority and responsibility for their own activities and function. The leaders of these units or groups may not be in senior roles, but instead are in leadership positions because of some expertise or experience that makes them the most appropriate leader. Distributed leadership may be a formal and strategic part of the structure of an organisation, such as in organisations that segment departments and projects as discrete business units, or it can emerge in response to circumstances (see the section later in this chapter on the links between reactions to the Covid-19 pandemic in some organisations and distributed leadership). Either way, by allowing responsibility and authority throughout an organisation, people can feel valued and enabled and consequently performance can be enhanced. There are also some challenges with regard to governance, line management and authority of course (see later in this chapter and the next for more on this). Broadly, though, there is clear resonance of distributed leadership with transformational techniques – distributed leadership involves person development and, in particular, *intellectual stimulation* can be a key part of this leadership approach. There are implied relational requirements too, including trust and respect and communication between leaders and followers vertically and laterally.

At its simplest: Distributed leadership distributes leadership roles throughout the organisation rather than just top-down.

Relational leadership

Relational leadership concerns reconceptualising what we mean by leadership, and as such it is a radical departure from how we have understood and practised leadership in the past. The core focus concerns a redefining of what leadership is, and positions it as emerging from the everyday interactions between the people who work throughout the roles represented in an organisation. It acknowledges that leadership may well still be part of a structured, even hierarchical, system, but it also allows and encourages that leadership emerges throughout organisations as a consequence of having people working together and relating to each other.

The philosophical underpinnings of relational leadership are presented in some detail by Lucia Crevani in Carroll et al.'s book on leadership (Crevani, 2019), and again the distinction between *headship* and leadership is important in the understanding of relational leadership – it moves the conversation away from leaders being the people who are appointed to designated posts, and refocuses attention on how leadership is continuously co-created in organisations via the relations between the people who work in them (see also Chapter 5). Given this focus on relationships, not unsurprisingly one of the key scholars in the development of this approach to understanding leadership is Mary Uhl-Bien (e.g. Uhl-Bien and Ospina, 2012), noted at the start of this chapter for her role in developing LMX (Graen and Uhl-Bien, 1995).

Most recently, in an editorial in 2021, the scholar Joe Raelin uses the term *collective leadership*, which develops the key ideas of relational leadership. He defines *collective leadership* as 'a dynamic co-constructed democratic process in which constellations of individuals working and making decisions together contribute knowledge, skills, and meaning to the tasks in hand'. As such, *collective leadership* is leadership that emerges from groups of people relating to each other and working together. It involves four key elements: *co-creation of leadership* amongst members of a team, *concurrent leadership* where more than one person at a time may be leading, *collaboration* between people and *compassion* for each other. Raelin (2021) proposes that this new focus is embodied in the term 'leaderful', which is applied to organisations that seek to engender a culture that acknowledges the value of relational leadership; organisations that seek to encourage and achieve a culture of support for people, mutuality and reciprocity between organisational and personal aims, and a holistic approach to developing people with compassion and empathy.

At its simplest: Relational leadership moves away from a focus on hierarchies and allows that leadership can also emerge via relations between people

Pluralist leadership in practice

While there has been much intellectual development in leadership knowledge since the beginning of the millennium, the practices of leadership reconceptualised as pluralist and emergent are in fact in their infancy in organisations. Some organisations have made attempts to redefine how leadership occurs, and some new organisations have adopted non-traditional systems of leading. In some cases, there have been good outcomes in terms of performance – two very high-profile examples are GoreTex and Gravity Payments, both in the USA.

GoreTex is a 50-year old company that manufactures apparel and other materials technologies. Gravity is a financial services company, started in 2004, that offers credit card processing. In both cases, flatter structures, explicit policies and organisational practices aimed at supporting and respecting people, and greater sharing of responsibility and authority, have been built into the organisational design and the business model. Both of these companies have achieved outstanding and prevailing performance results that they attribute to their organisational structures, and they both feature as case studies in articles and books about pluralist leadership (e.g. Manz et al., 2009 and Keegan, 2015, respectively).

More generally, though, there is limited research on the implementation of these newer ideas about and approaches to leadership in practice, as many organisations stick to older, tried and tested ways of leading, of developing leaders and of positioning leadership in organisational structures. As such, adoption of innovation and pluralism in leadership has not yet achieved a momentum in practice in organisations. However, cases and research that show the benefits in the modern world of pluralist approaches to leadership have not gone entirely unnoticed, but where it is applied there is often overlap with traditional ways of doing leadership in organisations. For example, along with colleagues, I present research in an article on distributed leadership in practice in a large law firm in the UK (Galloway et al., 2009). The research showcases the strategic and deliberate implementation of distributed leadership in the firm by the partners (in UK law firms the owners and board of directors are 'partners'). This involved distributing the leadership of client cases throughout the firm rather than the exclusive preserve of the senior team. Instead, on a rotation system everyone in the organisation was allocated leadership at some point or other. This included partners, lawyers, paralegals and even administrative staff, unheard of at the time in UK law firms. These measures had resulted in considerable benefits and returns for the firm, to the point where they had won awards for growth in financial performance that they attributed to their distributed leadership strategy and practices. However, the research also found that the distribution of leadership was largely an illusion; while leaders were observed throughout the organisation, in reality there remained a close monitoring from top management and so the partners were still very much in charge. As such, it was really *management by exception* that was being applied, involving intervention when necessary. That said, the firm realised significant value from enabling and supporting leadership throughout the hierarchy rather than top-down, and so motivation and engagement were optimised amongst the personnel who worked there and this was what drove the enhanced performance results. The hierarchical leadership structure was still intact, though, and so it was possible to monitor the various teams and distributed activities and intervene if things were going awry (see Chapters 2 and 3 on autonomy and management by exception).

PERSPECTIVES FROM PRACTICE 4.1

John Black is a station manager with one of the UK's fire and rescue services. More information about John can be found on page 2.

Trust is a central and essential component of each of the different ways of understanding leadership as relational, relating to community and pluralistic. Amongst the leaders who contributed testimony for this book, trust and distribution of responsibility emerged throughout. Even in directive mode, for example, John Black notes the need for trust and faith in the relationships throughout the hierarchy:

You would never, particularly in the emergency phase of an incident, doubt what somebody's telling you. You always take it as read. But that comes from the rank structure where you have the firefighters and the senior fire-fighters in charge at the very sharp end, a crew commander in charge of them, a watch manager in charge of them and I'm the station manager in charge of them all. And all the information would come up directly from the front line through to the strategic part of the incident where I am. All that information would be collated and re-evaluated if necessary. I personally wouldn't be in there [a fire] so if they find themselves in a dangerous position they would come on to the radio and say, 'I'm withdrawing because of ...', and you say, 'I agree with that, come on out', and then find out what the issue is and reattack it in a different way. If you had to withdraw you would withdraw. Equally, the other way, if you see them in a dangerous situation or you consider it to be dangerous you would withdraw them. And they would most certainly argue with you: 'We don't need withdrawn', and you say, 'No I want you withdrawn, get out of there and we'll find another form of attack on this fire.' And we do that on numerous occasions where I would be, 'Oh this is too dangerous, everybody out'. Because they are close to the fire, they can't see the dangers until they come out and then they realise what the dangers were. So they'll maybe resist but they do what they are told. And they respect and trust your decisions. So it relies very much on trust. I have to trust the firefighters and the firefighters have to trust me. But it wouldn't necessarily be face to face, it could be through two or three reporting lines before it reaches me.

Every other contributor leader also noted the criticality of trust and respect in their accounts of how they have achieved effective, successful leadership. Perhaps the principles of leadership as a community phenomenon have always been part of good leadership practice, only now being explored through philosophical and theoretical lenses with a view to capitalising on its potential for future gains in modern connected but dispersed organisational communities.

Perspectives from practice questions

1. To what extent do you think the reporting structures described by John represent distributed or shared leadership?
2. How important is the traditional senior leader (or incident commander) in an organisation like John's that distributes leadership roles? Would this be the same in other types of organisation?
3. Do you think that community and shared leadership will become more or less important in the future in private, public or third-sector organisations?

Critique of pluralist approaches to leadership

As noted, new pluralist ideas about leadership are receiving much attention amongst the research community and new theorising is developing. For practitioners, there are also burgeoning experiments and examples of new ways of developing leadership and new approaches to leading. There are several limitations already apparent, though. First, where there is distributed, dispersed or shared leadership, there is also an issue with identifying who has responsibility and authority. A lack of clear reporting lines is a problem in practical terms in most organisations and these new ideas have not yet resolved exactly how accountability and responsibility might be governed, leading to overlaps with older traditional methods, sometimes with a very formalised structure, as per John's testimony above, and even in the most pioneering companies, as per the Galloway et al. (2009) research. A further issue is that the reliance on relations between people can be inherently problematic, given the potential for cronyism and other types of favouritism that may transcend the effectiveness of a contribution to an organisation. Relationship-based approaches to leading also lend themselves to in-group/out-group mentality and competitiveness. While good relationships in working environments have been demonstrated many times to have benefits in terms of performance, the risk of toxic relationships, competitiveness and exclusion of good people because of their lack of social skills may be all too real in some organisations. Another risk is that the relationships act to stifle decision-making; if consensus has to be achieved, decisions that involve communities of practitioners will be slower. Meanwhile, the need to maintain good relationships between leaders and followers may stifle critical thinking as people seek to be agreeable rather than correct and are deterred from offering even constructive criticism. Equally, if there is a feeling of group monitoring, people may be less likely to act innovatively and creatively for fear of failure or ridicule or loss of face under surveillance. In practice in organisations these risks must be catered for if the asserted benefits of pluralist leadership are to be realised for future generations.

Two promising streams of research are developing to these ends and in both cases they involve taking a view of leadership that diverges from traditional top-down hierarchy approaches. The two recent development areas of potential importance in organisations are described as *leadership as process* and *leadership as practice* respectively, and both are summarised below.

LEADERSHIP AS PROCESS

Developmental work on understanding leadership as a process is focused on developing organisations rather than the individuals within them so as to achieve future goals and realise opportunities. Leadership is understood as a social and ongoing process in context, involving all parties contributing to organisational activities, direction and development. Understanding leadership as process therefore represents a move away from considering the immediate task in hand or even the things individuals are doing, and has a longer-term flavour to it whereby it is about developing an organisational culture where leading emerges as and when required and is conducted by the person or persons most suitable in terms of expertise and experience. This places any individual's leadership less as a role and more as a temporary state, as when conditions or priorities change, so too does the most appropriate person and approach to leading. In short, as Crevani et al. (2010) put it, leadership is positioned in an organisation as an ongoing and 'never ending story'.

Leadership as process is underpinned by recent work by Wilfred H. Drath and colleagues. In Drath et al. (2008) they present a model proposing direction, alignment and commitment (DAC) as a framework for enabling leadership as a process in organisations. This is summarised in Box 4.2.

Box 4.2: DAC

Direction: agreement of goals amongst members.

Alignment: the organisation and coordination of work between people.

Commitment: the prioritisation of the interests of the organisation above members' self-interests.

This DAC framework is intended to inform organisations with a view to managing some of the increasingly necessary collaborative ways of working in the modern connected world. The DAC framework is a lens through which an organisation can inspect and inform its culture so that it is able to meet the demands of the current dynamic peer-based, locally and globally networked economy.

Leadership as process thus concerns developing a culture in an organisation, where leadership, as a key part of that, is an ongoing and evolving process. As such there is resonance with the idea – outlined in Chapter 1 – that leadership is about more than just influencing the behaviours of others, but is also about *thought leadership* and the communication of that, the affordance of co-creation of organisational culture and goals amongst leaders and followers, and this being an ongoing, dynamic, iterative and reciprocal *process*.

At its simplest: Leadership as process proposes that leadership is not limited to people in roles but is understood as possible (and occurring) everywhere in organisations.

LEADERSHIP AS PRACTICE

A last means by which research is engaging with leadership is by exploring it through the *practices* of people within the cultural and structural environment of the organisation. As such, *leadership as practice* has as its focus not just the leader–follower relationships, but also actions and the ways in which leadership is enabled (Buchan, 2019). *Leadership as practice* refers to the interactions of people with the structures in an organisation; how people engage with these. As such, *leadership as practice* refers to reflexivity, which purports that people are influenced by their circumstances and contexts and in turn those circumstances and contexts are affected by a person's (and other persons') actions and activities.

Box 4.3: Reflexivity

Reflexivity concerns the dialectal relationship between agency and structure. It is a central pillar of a critical realist understanding of the world, espoused by theoreticians such as Margaret Archer (e.g. Archer, 1998). Reflexivity is the process by which a person is influenced by their circumstances, and vice versa. To summarise, an individual's actions and behaviours are influenced by things such as their background, skills, personality, experiences, etc. They are also influenced by context, such as the society they live in, the organisation they work for, the stability of the economy, etc. In turn, the individual is affected by his or her actions (for example they do things that develop new skills, achieve further experience, become wealthier). The individual has an effect on the context too (the workplace, for example, includes the activities and performance and outputs of that individual). Thus people's lives are affected by their contexts and, in turn, contexts are affected by the things people do in them. Understood as a reflexive process, it is not possible to understand individuals separate from their contexts and it is not possible to understand social or organisational life separate from the people who inhabit it. Cumulatively, therefore, social or organisational life develops by reflexive interaction between agents in contexts. It is how organisations and societies evolve – though incremental and myriad reflexive developments representing the interaction between the agency of individuals and the structures in which they live and work.

For approaches to understanding leadership that are focused on *leadership as practice*, it is the actions and outcomes of leadership that are the units of analysis. It is about what people actually do to lead (either in terms of work effort or in terms of communicating direction and new ways of doing things). So it is about their reflexive position in the organisation, their experiences, their backgrounds, their participation and how they are developed by and contribute to the development of the organisation. This requires that people are supported and enabled in organisations. This includes person-centric approaches to development, but it also includes the structural environment – including the processes, the policies and other bureaucracies – in place to enable people to lead and to support them when they do. For organisations, the key to developing leadership therefore lies in inspecting how well leading is supported and taking the steps required for enabling leadership practices throughout the organisation. The focus is therefore shifted from how to become a leader, to how to develop structures and people in organisations so that they can 'do' leadership. This will involve HR departments and C-suite executives, but it will also involve engagement and participation throughout organisations as processes and procedures are developed and embedded in working contexts. In the current, developing and future socio-economic and commercial world, consideration of leadership as practice will be essential for developing the ability to lead organisations and lead *in* organisations to engage with efficiencies and opportunities.

At its simplest: Leadership as practice focuses on the means and methods by which people are able to do leadership in organisations.

The global pandemic and new ways of leading

The global Covid-19 pandemic may well have speeded up some of the developments in approaches to leading in many organisations, as it forced a change in the ways people could be monitored and developed. Lockdowns in particular wrought radical changes in many organisations where working from home, flexible hours, greater tolerance of the domestic responsibilities of staff, and widespread delegation to a newly remote workforce substituted established on-site practices. Since the lockdown measures were considered by most organisations to be makeshift, temporary mitigations to maintain their business or function, it was largely considered these would be less effective than normal practice. But in fact a fascinating thing happened: rather than lose productivity, people stepped up. Lockdowns mandated by Covid-19 forced organisations to distribute work and leadership and afford greater autonomy to people. Rather than this resulting in organisational chaos and performance decline, in fact across industries and sectors, people rose to the challenges and hatched solutions, and kept the show on the road. The pandemic has been a global experiment in the effectiveness of distributed, shared, remote working, where people have acted autonomously to solve problems and achieve goals. Teachers developed ways of reaching students online without any previous training or precedent, so they could be taught and even awarded national qualifications. Administrators found ways to make systems work across international companies from kitchens and bedrooms. IT technicians fixed PCs and connected printers to laptops all over the world from their living rooms. These are just a few examples of the achievements that were not possible before the pandemic because in pre-Covid times traditional leadership approaches did not extend the trust and challenge required to do them. In a short time in virtually all industries the importance of presenteeism diminished and ways of monitoring and developing people changed radically. Rather than a loss of control or decreased performance, what has emerged is more leadership across and within organisations. The best organisations, the ones that will enhance their chances and future-proof their strategies, will not waste this accidental learning experience about the value of reconceptualising leadership.

PERSPECTIVES FROM PRACTICE 4.2

Priyanka Thali is a managing editor at CACTUS Communications, a technology company headquartered in India. More information about Priyanka can be found on page 3.

In her managing editor role, Priyanka Thali takes a perspective that is observably oriented towards sharing leadership. As she puts it:

> As a leader you are not the hero, you are somebody who is developing heroes ... My style involves identifying owners for things because what I've learned over the years is that delegation is one of the most important parts of your job. To do the stuff that I need to do I need to be able to develop a good team, so that I can develop better ideas, and so I can have a have things function more smoothly. So my approach has always been heavy on identifying owners and empowering my team to become owners. What I have come to do is have a team that's independent. I don't want a team that is dependent on me for everything. I want a team that functions like a well-oiled machine even in my absence. So that is where a lot of my time and effort goes – into fostering independent thinkers, people who are capable of making their own decisions, people who are confident and who can own their decisions ... For me, it's not just important for every team member to see themselves as self-reliant, the other members of the team and maybe even other teams should also see that person as somebody who's reliable and somebody who they can turn to. Others should see that person as someone who's important.

Perspectives from practice questions

1. Why do you think it is important for Priyanka to have staff who can take ownership?
2. Do you think there are benefits to an organisation like Priyanka's of having shared or distributed leadership?

SUMMARY: LEADERSHIP IN COMMUNITIES

This chapter has explored some of the newest knowledge that is still developing regarding leadership and leading in organisations. It summarises some of the key streams of research and practice that are moving away from focus on the individual leader as the traditional hero figure, and considering instead leadership as collective and pluralistic. For knowledge, there is implied a move away from examining the people in leadership roles, and consequently a greater distinction between headship and leadership, so that leadership – which can emerge anywhere in an organisation – is positioned as a phenomenon that drives direction, vision, knowledge and strategy.

The theory and practices of community/pluralist leadership are in their infancy. The implications for many organisations are not yet known. Leadership based on relationships and social networks presents a risk of favouritism and in- and out-group mentality. That said, early attempts to engage pluralistic approaches to leading have seen an advantage for some companies, and certainly it has piqued interest so that organisational profile has been raised in some cases, like Goretex and Gravity Payments. Meanwhile, as the testimonies of John as a fire-service leader and Priyanka as a managing editor attest, perhaps practice in pluralist and distributed forms of leadership are not as new as some theorists might think. The future of leadership will be interesting to watch as theory and practice develop in line with the needs of the next few years. There is no question that the need for new ways of looking at and doing leadership will not wane as the world becomes increasingly connected.

EXERCISES

What is your implicit leadership theory? Having read Chapters 1 to 4 do you think it has changed?

Consider your organisation or an organisation in which you have worked in the past. What is the leadership concept there? Do you think that was a help or a hindrance to organisational performance?

Summarise the types of pluralist approaches to leadership: shared, pooled, distributed. What are the distinctions between them?

Give an explanation of relational (collective) leadership.

Give an explanation of the core principles of leadership as process.

Give an explanation of the core principles of leadership as practice.

Can you think of any companies or other organisations that exhibit some form of pluralist leadership?

Reflect on your own life experience during the Covid-19 lockdown(s). Did you observe any organisations that were forced to do leadership in new ways? Did this involve distributing/sharing/devolving leadership?

Do you think that organisations have a more developed understanding about leadership and employee performance as a consequence of lockdowns and disrupted work practices during the Covid-19 pandemic in your industry, sector or country?

Do you think there are any advantages or disadvantages to retaining some of the distributed practices that were mandated for some organisations because of the pandemic?

5
LEADERSHIP CONTEXTS

From theory to practice

INTRODUCTION

Chapters 1 to 4 have outlined and summarised some of the evolution of knowledge on leadership. The following chapters turn to considering this knowledge as it is experienced and developed in practice in organisations. In this chapter, the challenges of leading in different circumstances and organisational contexts are explored. It is important at this stage to return to an earlier distinction – made in Chapter 1 – that leadership has two intersecting expressions. The first is to pioneer, to envision and to communicate that to others, what is referred to in this book as *thought leadership*. The second is to motivate and influence people so that they will contribute effort and action, referred to as *leading people*. Clearly, there is much overlap between these conceptualisations of leadership. Often a leader envisions a new idea and then has to find ways to make others commit and engage themselves in the actualisation of it. Equally, a leader of people often has to devise new ways of doing things and ideate solutions or opportunities. Despite this, they can also be discrete. For example, in organisations, a *leader of people* may not have any particular additional ideas and vision regarding strategic orientation or goals. Perhaps these are set by others in the hierarchy or elsewhere. But a leader must take them on and commit to them because a leader in organisational life will have a critical role in leading others to the achievement of them. On the other hand, *thought leaders* may have little direct contact with followers. *Thought leaders* are often those who pioneer, do things first, lead the way in terms of ways of thinking or of doing things. Public figures such as the climate crisis activist Greta Thunberg or the campaigner for education for girls Malala Yousafzai have no direct reports, yet they are often referred to as leaders because they have advocated a different way of doing things, departing from traditional ways or older or contentious knowledge. Elsewhere, though, leadership may involve smaller, less disruptive ideation – how to get things done, what processes to adopt to achieve goals. These require both *thought leadership* in the planning and envisioning, and *leading people* in terms of influencing efforts of others.

In this chapter, we will explore some contexts in which *thought leadership* and *leading people* occur. By exploring leadership in specific contexts, it is possible to link the theories and approaches discussed throughout the earlier chapters of this book with practice. First, the chapter will look at leadership and strategy and engage with the questions of how strategic leadership is done and why it is important. From there, three further example contexts are explored: *projects*, *creative industries* and *dynamic, high-stakes environments*. These examples are selected because of specific issues associated with leadership – project leaders tend to have little or no formal authority over the people they lead, leaders in creative industries must balance the ability to cultivate and develop creative people within commercial boundaries, and high-stakes leaders must lead in high-risk and constantly changing contexts. While the examples seem specific, the implications of them are quite wide, informing generally leadership in strategic, departmentalised, innovation-seeking, or dynamic contexts of practice respectively.

LEADERSHIP AND STRATEGY

Strategy is one of the most central and critical elements of all organisations, commercial, public or third sector. An organisation has to have leaders who know what they seek to achieve and have the ability to plan how to do it. Commercial organisations do not generate turnover or profits by accident. Similarly, third-sector and public organisations do not achieve their social, charitable or financial goals by accident. Goals are achieved by developing and executing strategies. There is a canon of knowledge about strategy and several firmly established theories, including Porter on competitive position, Miles and Snow's typology of approaches, and Mintzberg's distinction between long- and short-term orientation of organisations (Porter, 1985; Miles and Snow, 1978; Mintzberg and Waters, 1985, respectively). These are just a few of the most famous examples, and it is not the intention to explore these in detail here. Instead, the focus in this book is on how leadership may inform strategy and in turn, the role of leadership in executing it.

Let's explore first principles: ideas that become organisations have to start somewhere, and so too do ideas that contribute value to organisations. Someone has to have the vision and foresight to ideate a future goal, and thereafter a means by which to achieve that goal must be devised. This is likely to involve a mixture of both *thought leadership* and *leading people* in most organisations. Critically, though, in practice, this leadership may or may not come from one individual.

Entrepreneurs are often identified as commercial leaders, seen to enter markets with new ideas and disrupt – even revolutionise – them. This is especially true of the highest-profile entrepreneurs. Consider the *thought leadership* behind Microsoft and Amazon and Tesla and Alibaba. The names Bill Gates, Jeff Bezos, Elon Musk and Jack Ma immediately spring to mind. These four examples are almost universally considered to be leaders and, of course, in envisioning terms, they are. However, Microsoft, Amazon, Tesla and Alibaba did not become global giants on the strength of the original vision alone. The means by which to realise these visions was involved too, whether by these heroic figures, or by the teams around them. In addition, the original visions have since moved on – these entrepreneurial firms are the consequence of an original idea perhaps, but ongoing innovation and evolution of technology and new ideas have kept them competitive, and indeed, the current offerings in all of these companies bear little resemblance to the original propositions. Critically, this evolution involves far more people and their ability to envision and lead than the original founders. To achieve and maintain their status and performance all of these companies have structures in place to this day that afford ongoing ability to innovate and realise opportunities. While the founders may have influenced the organisational culture that was created and may well still participate and contribute, the culture prevails because leadership is happening throughout these organisations in an ongoing and strategic way.

Entrepreneurship thus goes beyond the founders of new companies that enter a market and disrupt it, such as the four examples above. Entrepreneurship is also a strategic position and an ongoing commitment in commercial organisations. In fact, of the four examples, Microsoft was started in 1975, Amazon in 1994, Alibaba in 1999 and Tesla in 2003 – hardly start-ups. Yet we consider them entrepreneurial still. This is because they continue to act entrepreneurially, and this is strategic.

According to the entrepreneurial leadership scholar Christian Harrison, a leader must be able to recognise and exploit opportunities and be able to take risks. This describes how we think about entrepreneurs generally, but Harrison (2018) notes that this principle applies to leadership throughout organisations too. Leaders throughout hierarchies are able to perceive or envision opportunities and use influence to exploit them. Those at the top of management structures will have the broadest view, while others dispersed throughout the hierarchy may have more specialist perspectives.

The most successful organisations have created a culture of strategy and leadership that enables the creation of vision and influences people to contribute to the co-creation of the operating environment that will realise it. For corporate and other private enterprises, recent research on what theorists such as Schoemaker et al. (2018) refer to as *dynamic capabilities* of firms underlines the importance of understanding leadership more broadly than just referring to the top management or the C-suite. In the complex, turbulent and fast-paced market environments of most competitive industries, a commercial organisation's reaction times and ability to seize opportunities – its *dynamic capabilities* – are critical to survival and success. The entrepreneurial organisation must be alert to both opportunities and to competitive and other pressures, and critically, the leaders in these organisations must have means by which they may create or seize opportunities or mitigate threats. An organisation in context is complex and the bigger the organisation the greater the complexity. For leaders, therefore, the more sophisticated their knowledge and understanding of complex environments, the better an organisation will fare. The ability to vision, communicate and execute responses to opportunities or threats is therefore not optimally confined to the few.

Linking theory to practice

For commercial organisations all over the world, strategy may be focused on maintaining market position or on growing it. Research has shown that for either scenario, organisations must strategise. Here we will focus on growth strategy, as appropriate for a textbook on leadership for developing careers and organisations. The focus is private or corporate commercial firms, but the principles apply equally to third-sector organisations and there are clear implications too for public sector leaders.

There are three ways to grow a firm:

1. Increase the number of things you offer (increase range).
2. Increase the number of people who buy your offering (increase market).
3. Do both.

While the description may be simple, the achievement of growth is not, and there are countless books and articles and research studies exploring ways to manage and achieve it in different industries and locations. Important here is the role of leadership. To lead with a view to organisational growth, leadership must be mindful of organisational culture and must be able to generate a vision of the idea or future. This will be optimally enabled by having as much contribution and exchange of knowledge as possible and so lines of communication throughout the organisation must allow for efficient flows of information *into* the strategy. Once decisions are made, the vision or idea must be 'sold' throughout the organisation so that others can subscribe to it and so that they can work towards achieving, advocating and making contribution to it through work effort and through their own ideas and emerging leadership. From an organisational strategy point of view, there are three key enablers:

1. The greater organisational strategy must be clear to participants throughout the organisation so that they can subscribe and contribute.

2. Means of communicating contributions must be accessible.
3. Risks that limit the generation and communication of ideas must be minimised, including operating a 'no-blame' culture.

In summary, leadership must communicate, enthuse, enable and support. Leaders who seek to grow or otherwise develop organisations must personalise the mission, and connect with and inspire the team who will deliver it. That will vary depending on the job at hand and the people involved and so there is resonance with context-based theories of leadership and the need for leaders to consider and adapt their approaches according to context. Thereafter, respect, trust and value will motivate participation. The links with transformational approaches to leadership are clear (consider the role of the four I's – see Chapter 3). The links with relational forms of leadership are also clear. Transactional leadership approaches will form part of this culture too, with rewards and incentives (intrinsic and extrinsic) built in. But newer thinking about leadership is also relevant here as the organisational cultures best suited to enabling meaningful contribution are those that can, in effect, facilitate the emergence of leadership (thought-based and influence-based) throughout an organisation. At the same time, though, in commercial organisations there is a need to manage this culture and the processes in it. Rowe (2001) categorises three types of leadership, *visionary*, *strategic* and *managerial*, broadly representing *thought leadership*, *leading people* and the more structured administrative functions of *management* (see Chapter 1). Rowe notes that in entrepreneurial organisations all three of these functions are required for success.

PERSPECTIVES FROM PRACTICE 5.1

Jannie Tam is the founder of the Hong Kong-based talent development company GROWDynamics. More information about Jannie can be found on page 1.

John Black is a station manager with one of the UK's fire and rescue services. More information about John can be found on page 2.

Claire McCarthy is the Director of Operations and HR at a large children's charity in Wales. More information about Claire can be found on page 2.

Priyanka Thali is a managing editor at CACTUS Communications, a technology company headquartered in India. More information about Priyanka can be found on page 3.

Jannie Tam explains the need for entrepreneurs to communicate that a start-up is going places to keep people engaged and invested:

(Continued)

[As an entrepreneur/founder] your colleagues are either under you or work with you. I have no boss to report to. You must try to embed their aspirations, and you also have to make sure that your business is growing, even if it's slow. Because no one will wait forever. If it is a small organisation and the growth is not happening, you will lose people. Because they also want to see that they can grow with the business and no one can wait and wait. So the growth comes from better revenues, better partnerships, and people will need to see something is happening. So I think as a leader you just need to demonstrate your perseverance and you have to create some exciting news, exciting prospects ... to make them feel like OK it is still something that is moving and growing. Nowadays job security is hard to find; even in big organisations, there's so many redundancies and fewer jobs now because of Covid. But some people can still create something out of the difficult situation. And for others you have to demonstrate you are not gonna give up. But that doesn't mean that I stick to the old tricks. I need to modify things, reflect the changes in the market and that doesn't stop. I bring some of the challenges to them so as a team we have to find ways to crack the situation. So they're not just blindly following someone. They also feel like they can contribute their thinking; that is important.

Jannie refers specifically to her entrepreneurship. Her assertion of the need to inject ideas from colleagues and afford them a sense of ownership of the strategic aims of her firm is echoed by Victor in the multi-national corporation he works in too, though in his case it is specifically enabled in the organisational structure and procedures. He explains:

Where you're shaping up the opportunity and you're coming up with the delivery strategy to deliver that project the workshop style normally works very well with the wider team in terms of brainstorming and pulling together ideas. As you can appreciate, there are also quite a few experienced people around the table, and so you want to make sure you're pulling in that experience where possible, and both regionally and globally as well. So that is the kind of shape it takes. It's a very formal process most of the time in the organisation where you run a sort of a chattering session of some sort, where you shape that strategy and make sure that it gets fed into the delivery plan of the project so you can set the vision.

John Black relates a similar approach to strategising, but this time in a public service context:

We meet up regularly and not only with the watch managers but meet up regularly with the crews themselves and disseminate any information down and take questions. It is very important to make the strategy clear and as

things develop ... And in terms of community engagement and fire preven-
tion, the [greater organizational] strategy broadened out from us being
there to save lives, to saving lives before an event happened. And the idea
was that we would save lives by going out and fitting smoke detectors for
vulnerable people. We go to fires in the same household involving the same
people on a regular basis and these people are very vulnerable because it
is only a matter of time before they really hurt themselves or people around
them. These people became targets. But we have a lot of unknown people
who basically slip under the radar. So we have had to develop a strategy
for dealing with people we couldn't find, for the vulnerable and disaffected
people. So it was very important that all of this was discussed with the fire
crews that worked in and knew the communities. And it was a discussion
as opposed to 'this will be the strategy'. To achieve these aims we have
proper discussions with the watch managers, the line managers and the
crews themselves.

As noted in Chapter 3, Claire McCarthy advocates inclusion in ideation and implementation of strategy too in her charity context. Priyanka Thali notes in particular the need for
people to understand where they fit in the value chain of a strategic aim of the organisation. In her role as a publisher, she notes of her team that:

They need to be aware of the organisation's goals. They need to know
what they're working towards and what part they're playing in it. So it can't
just be like, 'OK, I tell you to do this, and then you do this'. They need to
understand why they're doing certain things. They need to understand
what is in it for them. And that's how I try to foster ownership of tasks. So
it's not just about you doing it because you're meant to do it, but you are
responsible for this. You own this and this is how it will benefit the organisation as well as you.

Perspectives from practice questions

1. Why is it important to Jannie that her team feel part of the development of
   GROWDynamics?
2. Why do you think it is important for her team to feel that Jannie has plans for the
   development and growth of the firm?
3. Why is it important that Victor and John are inclusive about setting the strategy and
   vision in their respective examples?
4. Does the variation between their sectors (private and public) affect the reasons for
   inclusivity?
5. Why do you think Priyanka asserts that people need to understand how their work
   fits with the strategy and goals of the organisation? Do you see any links with some
   of the motivations theories outlined in Chapter 1?

LEADERSHIP AND CREATIVITY

Creative industries include those involving art, design, performance, composition, but in fact creativity is required in all industries to some degree. Problem solving always requires a degree of creativity, and for an organisation that seeks to foster innovation, enabling and supporting creativity are especially critical. In charitable or public organisations this must be done within the confines of, and compliant with, financial and budgetary parameters. In commercial organisations, the ability to profit is a further priority. The issue for leaders, therefore, is how to enable creativity so that it makes a value-adding contribution to an organisation, but contain it too. The scenario in Box 5.1 exemplifies the challenge.

Box 5.1: Creative versus commercial interests

Let's take the example of a medium-sized photography firm. The revenues for this firm come from two main sources. The first, Activity A, is its specialism in landscape photography for clients which serves provenance-oriented markets, such as food and drinks firms and the tourism and hospitality sector that use these images for advertising purposes. The second main revenue stream, Activity B, is contracts with local authorities to take annual individual and group school photographs. There is a third activity too, Activity C: the firm showcases its quality and artistic credentials by hosting and contributing to photographic exhibitions. This is used as a means by which to profile the business and the quality of its offering amongst the photography and media community.

Most of the photographers in this firm join in order to develop in and contribute to Activity A, and most hope one day to contribute to Activity C. Indeed, the reputation of the firm is built on its style and artistry in these activities. However, the schools contract is lucrative and the income from it supports the ability to fund the more aesthetic pursuits of A and C. There are two key tensions here, though. First, all the photographers in the firm want to do the landscape work rather than the school work. Second, some require escalating amounts of resources, such as personnel, light, equipment, etc., to create landscape images of spectacular beauty. For the senior management of the firm, there is a balance to be struck in terms of maintaining income, quality in all activities, developing reputation for excellent art and ensuring cost-effectiveness.

Similar to the circumstances in Box 5.1, along with a colleague, I conducted a study of similar issues amongst a sample of architecture firms (Galloway and Haniff, 2015). This research not only explored the tensions of leading in creative environments, but also focused on these issues in the specific contexts of projects, exploring how these were managed and led while maintaining conditions that were stimulating and motivating for creative workers. The section below looks at leading in projects in more detail, but more generally, similar to the photography example, the tensions emerging concerned the need for the architecture firms to develop creativity but within commercially feasible parameters. In particular, the need to afford opportunities to create designs of aesthetic interest and even beauty for buildings sat alongside the need to fulfil contracts for more routine work, such as designing functional, affordable municipal buildings. In terms of leading in creative industries, or any circumstance in organisations where innovation or problem solving or new ideas are important, there is a need for leaders to reflect on and consider carefully how to extract best creative effort in a cost-effective way that affords development of both the individual and the organisation.

Practical implications include that it can be useful to allow people autonomy and discretion in order to get the best from them – to allow them to express their creativity, try new things, experiment and develop. At the same time, some focus and incentivisation of business objectives is required too. So leadership that enables creativity may be most effective when it comprises a person-centric approach that affords people creative autonomy, but exercises some control over the extent to which that may occur within the parameters of business objectives and constraints. Unless creatives are allowed to flourish and develop, though, there will be no innovation. That is fatal for an organisation in a creative industry, and will stifle growth in any other industry. Equally, unrestrained pursuit of art can be reckless and counterproductive for an organisation in survival terms too.

Linking theory to practice

Theories about leadership suggest that for creative people to really flourish, they should be enabled to work autonomously, be trusted to do a good job, be encouraged to try new things and develop new techniques. These are suggestive of consensual, supportive, even laissez-faire approaches to leading, with a suggestion also of the importance of relational qualities, such as trust and value and respect, required of quality autonomous work. The inspirational and supportive features of transformational leadership are also recognisably informative here too, as people are encouraged to develop and excel and, indeed, there is resonance with the sharing and distribution of leadership too as people are enabled to pioneer and prospect. At the same time, though, there is a balance to be struck with commercial interests, and so while these techniques are critical for the development of quality and creativity, so too is there a need to manage and lead people in line with budgets. Means by which this balance may be struck by leaders include the affordance of equality of opportunity and distribution of different types of work amongst those working in the organisation. Another approach might be to have people work on more than one service at a time so that each may experience the range of work required by the organisation in the competitive environment. However developed, the role of leaders is to manage and balance the tension between being progressive as a creative organisation and budget-compliant or profit-based as an economic one. This requires consideration and reflection from leaders, including the ideation associated with *thought leadership* and the influence needed for *leading people* effectively and commensurate with the organisation's ambitions.

PERSPECTIVES FROM PRACTICE 5.2

Claire McCarthy in the children's health service charity notes the tension as a director of operations with dealing with the creative people in her organisation. First though, she notes:

> I've always argued that in the back-office systems there's a lot creativity as well. So if you're going to build a decent process to manage all that wonderful income that their advertising is going to bring in you have to be quite creative sometimes. I think that you have to be quite creative in most forward-thinking organisations whatever department you happen to be in.

> We've got fundraisers and marketeers and people who you know have to design and make things appealing and attractive, though, and one of the things I try to do is evidence to the creative people the value of the back-end operations being a party to the conversation right from the get-go. It's great they're having all these wonderful ideas but how on earth are we going to process that? I think if you're able to collaborate quite well with the more creative side of the business they soon see a value in you … to the point now where my creatives will always include me in the initial planning because they know that at some point, I'm going to have to get the income they're bringing in channelled to their coding. Ultimately their coding is going to show whether they've achieved their objectives or not and if I can't code it properly then they're not going to see that reflected in the accounts, all the work that they have done. So you can evidence to them that you're on board with them, you are as excited about this campaign as they are, and that you will try and troubleshoot as much as you can to make sure that the fulfilment process, the pre-sales, the after sales, are all complementing, you are all working to the same aim, to the same outcome.

Perspectives in practice questions

1. Why do you think Claire seeks to be involved in the conversations about the creative parts of campaigning and marketing the charity?
2. What do you think would be the outcomes if the creatives in the children's charity did not have to consult with Claire?
3. What do you think Claire means when she says that all staff in 'forward-thinking' organisations have to be creative?

LEADERSHIP AND PROJECTS

The project management scholar David Cleland describes projects as often cross-functional, and sometimes including multiple people matrixed from different parts of the organisation or external to it. People join project teams on a temporary basis with a particular remit, oftentimes in a purely transactional process (Cleland, 1995). Certainly, some projects operate just like this, with specialist, sometimes external, personnel injected in, paid and then moved on to the next job. On first sight, therefore, projects appear to be ideally suited to managerial or transactional leadership since they are considered task-focused and time-bound with specific budgets; the classic project management triad of time, cost and quality. The key problem for those who lead projects is their lack of legitimate power though. Project leaders in the main have no authority in terms of pay, promotion or punishment. They can neither incentivise nor penalise. So, in fact, there is little extrinsic means of transaction available to them. Projects are thus, at least to some extent, often staffed by employees or contractors who require other types of motivation and leadership. With no authority or power to affect pay, rewards or penalties, the project leader appears to be left with limited means of motivating people so that they may contribute their efforts.

Critical to project leadership, according to the project management specialist Aaron Shenhar, is the need for a leader to encourage engagement amongst project team members by sharing the vision and inspiring people to work on its realisation. This sharing and advocating the vision is only possible if the project leader – and the project team members – understand how the project fits in the greater organisational strategy. Shenhar (2004) refers to the concept of *strategic project leadership* as a means by which organisations that use projects might optimise performance by communicating between the hierarchies, including in projects, so that everyone knows how their efforts fit and what role and value they have to the greater strategic goals of the organisation. From there a project leader may devise an appropriate strategy for leading his or her team, commensurate with the overall corporate strategy and goals.

In their book on project leadership, Burke and Barron (2007) note that while a project team is often understood as a resource, leadership to encourage excellence will maintain focus on team members as individuals, able to add value if encouraged and motivated. While this suggests transformational techniques, these opportunities can also be seen to be transactional. A leader in these circumstances might give project members challenging work, the opportunity to develop skills or develop experiences that may improve access in the future to other projects and areas of work, or even contribute to overall development that may be useful for promotion and reward in the future. These are offered in exchange for engagement and effort. At the same time, though, they are also transformational as they are people-centred, individualised and developmental.

Linking theory to practice

The project management specialists Rodney Müller and Ralf Turner refer to leadership in projects as requiring key competencies ranging from critical analysis and vision to sensitivity and conscientiousness – all resonant with transformational leadership techniques (Müller and Turner, 2007, 2010). While there are various competencies associated with different projects in different industries and sectors (and that thus resonate with context-based theories), an overarching summary includes that project leadership has four key stages (Müller and Turner, 2010). These are outlined in Box 5.2.

Box 5.2: Four key stages for leading in projects

1. Understand the project goal

The project leader should understand the overall mission and the component part the project plays in it. S/he is thus enabled to develop an informed plan of how the project will be achieved within the cost, time, quality scope.

2. Personalise it

The project leader should take on the aims and goals of the project and envision ways of making them happen. Thus, the leader invests and engages personally and this allows him/her to communicate the aims and scope well – even enthusiastically – so that members may engage too.

3. Connect with the team

A project leader should make a point of knowing the team members – their names, their professional backgrounds and expertise, their work and career ambitions, their external talents and interests. This knowledge will inform the ability to provide opportunities and experiences that will be tailored and valuable for members. In gaining this knowledge, there will be exchange in terms of members' opinions and comments about the project, its aims and its operations, and these too may be valuable.

4. Conduct the project

The project leader should assign people to appropriate tasks, as informed by knowing them and their aspirations. In addition, the leaders should delegate responsibility and authority, encourage ideas and autonomy, operate a no-blame culture, lead by example and participate. The need to represent the team in other parts of the management structures of the organisation is critical to enabling the trust required for effective project leadership.

In concert with the principles in Box 5.2, Prabhakar (2005) also recommends transformational leadership techniques for projects. As with any environment that could be described as low authority, there is an emphasis in projects on team building. For project managers specifically, they must demonstrate competence in the project purpose, efficiency in using project techniques and leadership of the people who make up the project team. It is the project leader who resolves conflicts and manages expectations amongst stakeholders at the start of the project. It is the project leader who develops the project's strategy for goal achievement. And it is the project leader who motivates the different members of the team to deliver project success.

As Box 5.2 illustrates, while the tools of leadership that are available to line managers are not usually available to project leaders, there are other ways to lead effective and successful projects. In particular, while the extrinsic rewards usually reserved for those with headship roles or otherwise official authority within an organisation are largely not available to those who lead projects, transactional leadership is still possible. The opportunity to do challenging work, build skills and experience, work on tasks one enjoys, these are all often within the gift of a project leader. At the same time, the overlaps with transformational techniques are clear: consider the need to inspire, through enthusiasm and conduct, the benefits of providing support and stimulation, and from a transformational and relational point of view, a project leader may well have good knowledge of the people in his or her team and tailor these opportunities accordingly. The distributed and temporary nature of projects also comprises inherent suggestion of distribution of leadership and diversity in terms of team members (followers) and different strategic and operational purposes. There is resonance in this respect too therefore of an appropriate fit to situational and contingent approaches to leadership.

PERSPECTIVES FROM PRACTICE 5.3

Victor Ikande is a regional head for the US-based construction firm Hollins. More information about Victor can be found on page 3.

Victor Ikande describes his take on the challenges of leading in projects in construction:

> If it's a matrix organization like we have, where you might have line management responsibility but not the project responsibility for people, quite often people are in contact with somebody else on a day-to-day basis. And there's always a problem if a project manager is more task oriented, and they are just drilling people to get what they need, and then send them back when they're done and the line manager can console them and make sure they are

(Continued)

motivated. And that's a very prevailing culture unfortunately in organizations where the project management is different from the line management ...

I am both a line manager and a project manager, but in the past when I wasn't a line manager, I tried to make sure that I told people if I thought they were doing great. I also made it obvious to whoever was responsible for delivering that person's career objectives so they were aware of that. And so the person feels that while I'm not responsible for promoting you directly, I care about your career. And that worked a trick and really helped and quite often I would deliberately go push if I felt somebody was due a promotion. There's also this strategy where there's a next role for a person and you try to give them experience for that role in the project. So you don't see them purely as a resource into your project. You start working with them towards achieving some career goals for the next level. And those are ways that work effectively. If they tell you that they want to go to the next level as a project manager, you go, 'OK, I'll start giving you PM responsibilities now so that when you have your conversations with your line manager you have the ammunition', and in the background you are also doing some lobbying on their behalf where possible – putting in a good word for them.

Priyanka Thali conducts much of her work with teams that come together from across departments. She outlines the issues thus:

Influencing people from other departments to work towards shared goals, that is a challenge. It could be a managing editor from a different department and an operations manager and a client manager, so different sorts of hierarchies there ... I think the problem lies with the fact that we have a different set of values probably, and we haven't had the opportunity to know each other, on a closer level. So I think lack of context is one barrier, because I may not know what context that person has been working in and vice versa. And then there will be differences of opinion and things like that, different perceptions. I think these are things that are barriers when it comes to influencing across departments. We try to overcome that by having conversations.

Claire McCarthy enjoys leading projects in her third-sector organisation where appropriate, and notes that they can help with organisational leadership more generally:

With a project, it's just much more focused than an ongoing leadership role. So you can see a beginning, a middle and an end to it. And it can be quite good because you are going to see an outcome, whereas other things are just trundling along. Projects bring people together. You use a little bit of flattery you know: 'You're here for a reason, we think that you've got something to give to this project.' People like that especially if they feel that maybe they've got a hidden talent that hasn't been noticed. So they can quickly get engaged because they think, 'Oh I've been picked for this, I'm somebody they want for this'. I think it can give a bit of confidence to people. But you do have to explain on the first meeting why they are all here. I think until people see that they're there for a reason, that they've been picked for a reason and that this isn't just for the sake of it, I think if people see a purpose, they get involved especially if that purpose is going to have a direct impact on their day job.

Perspectives from practice questions

1. Do you have experience of projects in which people were expected to perform and leave, as Victor describes? How did that affect motivation?
2. To what extent do you think Victor's strategy of influencing people in his projects was transactional or transformational?
3. Why do you think it is important for Priyanka to have conversations with people when she is on cross-departmental jobs?
4. Why do you think Claire finds leading temporary projects useful for her leadership?
5. Do you think it is appropriate that Claire 'flatters' the people she selects to work in projects with her? Why do you think she does this?
6. Why do you think people engage with projects in Claire's charity especially well when they think it will affect the greater organisation?

LEADERSHIP IN DYNAMIC, HIGH-STAKES ENVIRONMENTS

Circumstances that are dynamic and high risk are where there is greatest need of strong and effective leadership, according to scholars such as Boin et al. (2016) writing about emergency responses to crises. Dynamic, high-stakes environments describe situations where there are risks to safety, health and lives, but include too any circumstances where the situation is dynamic and risks are high, including to things such as property or quality of offering. Consequently, medical emergencies, military combat situations and emergency services rescue responses are all examples of where leadership must account for dynamic environments and high stakes, but so too are busy commercial kitchens, for example, where the whole value proposition relies on fast, quality service and performance, made more complex by the need for efficient safety measures and procedures. For these sorts of circumstances key elements of leadership include competence, reliability and flexibility in terms of being able to envision and envision again as circumstances change.

Writing about emergency medicine in particular, Shanahan et al. (2020) add that the ability to stay calm, keep a clear head and be alert to ongoing unanticipated changes in the situation are also key.

Linking theory to practice

In teams that routinely deal with fast, high-stakes circumstances trust comes into play in a very clear way. Often there is substantial pre-planning, rehearsal and practice of simulated scenarios, and these activities can be critical in real emergency situations; they test the structures that dynamic, high-stakes leadership relies on, the chains of command and communications procedures necessary in an emergency, all of which have to be well established before the emergency occurs. So for teams that exist, at least in part, to provide emergency response, communication lines must be pre-established, clear and effective. Thereafter, members of the team should know who does what, when and why. This is all suggestive of a directive, even autocratic, approach (see Chapter 2). However, recent research has found also that there are advantages to taking more dynamic approaches to leadership in dynamic situations. For example, the person in overall charge may relinquish control where necessary so that specialists may lead as appropriate to circumstances, and resonant with the principles outlined in Chapter 4 on shared and distributed leadership, there may be shifts in leadership throughout an emergency situation. In a paper on emergency obstetrics, for example, Mesinioti et al. (2020) present research that finds that leadership is discursively achieved in emergency circumstances, as different specialists take the lead interchangeably as circumstances dictate. Mesinioti et al. observe that these subtle changes in leadership occur as a result of verbal and non-verbal signals in the dynamic environment. This is not possible without trust. It is also not possible unless the person who is officially in charge is able to understand that in these sorts of circumstances, leadership may include *relinquishing control* when necessary and resuming it as the situation allows.

Other dynamic, high-stakes environments may be more complex again. For example, in circumstances of crisis, such as a terrorist attack, natural disaster or other catastrophic event, there may be multiple different agencies involved. According to Waugh (2018), the greater the complexity of the situation, the greater the potential ambiguity about who is in charge – who is the leader? While in many countries, governments, military agencies and emergency response bodies do conduct multi-agency scenario planning and simulations, the point is that dynamic, high-stakes environments are by definition loaded with the potential for the unanticipated and unexpected to occur in situations that are continually changing. For leaders, there is a need to:

- know who has overall authority, what the chains of command are amongst leaders and personnel throughout the situation, and how the communications between these work;

- achieve team compliance with authority and leadership throughout the chain of command;
- be able to understand and deal with complexity;
- understand and deal with changes in circumstances in real time;
- make fast, clear decisions calmly.

In essence, therefore, leading in dynamic, high-stakes environments involves being calm and able to make informed and important decisions in what can appear (and even be) chaotic circumstances.

PERSPECTIVES FROM PRACTICE 5.4

John Black explains how the structural operational model of a fire and rescue service works to enable leadership, including in emergency response situations:

The rank structure within the stations consists of the station manager and then we have four watches within each station who cover the whole period of a week. And within that watch structure is a watch manager who looks after the whole watch personnel. And below him is a crew manager who looks after crewmen or firefighters at a fire. All this is designed in order to dovetail in with our operational requirements. For example, a crew manager will be in charge of four firefighters within a sector of a fire and a watch manager will be in charge of anything up to four sectors and the station manager will be in charge of the overall operation and logistics and strategy of dealing with any type of incident. He will be the incident commander unless for some reason a higher-ranking officer is required to attend.

The way the structure is ranked like that is in order that it can be identified easily and quickly what everyone's role is and what level of responsibility that person can have, whether it be in charge of 4 people or 16 people or the whole fire incident itself. We need all that to be very clear for safety reasons. It was identified by some research that an incident officer could only reasonably have two or three spans of control to maintain safety and operational efficiency of the incident. So an incident commander without having the rank structure at an incident would be responsible for somewhere in the teens of spans of control which is overloading the incident commander's ability to think sharply and clearly. So some of the responsibilities are disseminated down to other ranks who can make quick sharp small decisions based on a strategic vision that is disseminated from the station commander to the watch managers to the crew managers to the firefighters themselves. And

(Continued)

that's the same organisation and structure that we use within a station for normal administration when we are not attending fires; we try to replicate both management systems within a normal working environment and at a high-pressure incident. In that way everyone is familiar with the structure and in an emergency incident it's very clear who does what.

Perspectives from practice questions

1. Why do you think it is useful that the fire and rescue service John works in has a single organisational structure for emergency and non-emergency context work?
2. How important do you think pre-defined reporting structures are in other types of dynamic, high-stakes circumstances? Consider for example, an operating theatre, a lifeguarding situation, a subsea pipe maintenance task, or a busy restaurant kitchen?

SUMMARY

This chapter has explored some of the ways in which leadership can and does play out in practice. It refers to both *thought leadership* and *leading people* and the overlaps between these. In organisations both are needed, but it would be almost impossible for any single person to inhabit all the leadership requirements (and management) for success in most organisations. As such, the credibility of the heroic single leader seems undermined by observable practice in most cases. That said, many organisations do have their figureheads and often these are the founders or entrepreneurs or leaders or officers in charge who have shaped the organisational culture so that more leading may emerge.

This chapter has also explored how important leadership is in terms of formulating strategy and executing it, and, in turn, the role of strategy in informing how leading might optimise performance is identified as critical. Three example contexts of where there are particular challenges for leaders – creative contexts, project contexts and dynamic, high-stakes contexts – serve to illustrate the wider issues associated with leading in different types of environments. Throughout, there are links with theory to be drawn and it is clear that theory and extant knowledge about leadership that has developed over decades has a role to play in informing and shaping practice. The challenge for leaders is the reflection and consideration of the means by which the goals of an organisation, the teams within them and the individuals throughout can be facilitated and optimised through leadership practice.

EXERCISES

Outline the key issues associated with strategic leadership.

Give an explanation of the key issues associated with leading in creative contexts.

Can you think of any other example industries or types of organisation that would have to balance the tensions associated with simultaneously leading within commercial parameters but encouraging creativity?

Consider the photography firm example scenario in Box 5.1. If you were the owner/CEO of this firm how would you:

a.   distribute work?
b.   encourage the development of art?

Do you consider strategic leadership and leadership in creative contexts to require leadership at the top only or throughout the organisation?

Give an explanation of the challenges of leading in projects and other low-authority contexts.

Consider an experience of working in a project or matrixed team. How well led was it? What, if anything, would you do differently?

Give an explanation of some of the things that can be done in advance to help efficient leadership in a dynamic, high-stakes environment?

6
LEADING AND DIVERSITY

As noted in earlier chapters of this book, even though we know traits and stereotypes are not necessarily good predictors of leadership, in many organisations notions about leaders prevail – what they look like and what they do – as the *implicit leadership theories* and *leadership concepts* described in Chapter 4. In organisations therefore, it can still be the case that, despite current knowledge and understanding about leadership, there is a specific aspirational model of it, and to advance through the hierarchical structure, some compliance with this model may be required. As we have noted in Chapters 1 and 4, what is described in most career and promotion structures is advancement into *headship* roles rather than *leadership* per se. Nevertheless, most organisations refer to this as their *leadership structure*, and indeed, it seems reasonable to expect some competence in leadership amongst those assigned to the roles.

Meanwhile, most advancement brings with it, at least on paper, increased responsibility and work, and is subject to greater expectations from those above and below in the organisational hierarchy. This is the rationale that underpins corresponding uplifts in pay and conditions – the higher one advances, the better the pay and reward – classic notional transactions. Inherent in this rationale of better pay and conditions in exchange for increased responsibility and effort is the presumption that the priorities of the organisation accord with the lifestyle of the individual. Thus, the bestowing of leadership roles in organisations – while one would hope skills and competence play a part – in practice also may involve conformity with an organisation's *leadership concept* and an expectation of an ability and willingness to fit within the context of existing organisational structures.

Where we have archetypes and expectations of leadership, though, there is an obvious disadvantage for any people who do not *fit* in some way. In this chapter we explore one of the key discrepancies found in leadership studies, that of the distribution of leadership roles amongst different groups. Gender is explored in some detail in the sections that follow and there are two reasons for this. First, in every country there are fewer women in leadership positions than men, most often in public life and consistently in commercial organisations. Second, and clearly related to the first, there has been much comment and systematic research on the differences in rates of leadership between men and women, so we have substantial evidence with regard to some of the potential reasons why this is the case and the effects this difference has on individuals, organisations and economies. Diversity refers to far more than just gender, though, and a body of knowledge is developing that is exploring diversity and leadership with a focus on, for example, ethnic minorities in various countries, sexual orientation, (dis)ability and health, and socio-economic status. In their book on leadership and diversity, Syed and Ozbilgin (2019) summarise much of this work. Here we take the example and most ubiquitously under-represented group – women – to explore some of the issues associated with diversity and leadership; however, the broad principles that apply to gender can often also apply in a wider sense to relate to diversity more generally.

VARIATION IN LEADERSHIP BY GENDER

There have been many studies over the last few decades that have explored whether there is variation between the effectiveness of male and female leaders. For example, Place and Vardeman-Winter (2018) summarise literature in the public relations field, concluding that when other factors are constant, there is no variation in leadership effectiveness by gender. Mirchandani (1999) found similar two decades before in the entrepreneurship field. Other meta-analyses show consistency with this across studies, organisations and geographies (e.g. Paustian-Underdahl et al., 2014 and Gipson et al., 2017). There is, however, some evidence that *styles* of leading may vary by gender.

The blurry qualities of *feminine* and *masculine* have been given binary status in most cultures in the world, and certain traits and behaviours have been attributed to one or the other. This has leaked from society and cultural life into organisational life, and to specific types of roles within organisations. Leadership is one of these. Research has helped clarify the situation from an evidence-based point of view in recent years. Men and women are part of the socio-culture and as such there is argument that they learn to act in ways that align with expectations and idealisations; they *conform* to their gender category at least to some degree, and in this way gender is *performative*. The notion of performativity is central to the work of the social and political philosopher Judith Butler who theorises that we perform gender roles in line with socio-cultural norms and expectations (Butler, 1990). Elsewhere, though, there are socio-cultural beliefs and support for the idea that gender – and therefore characteristics associated with men and women – is biologically *determined*. In fact, for our purposes here, it makes no difference if neither, either or both of these are correct. The fact remains that through-out the world women and men tend to approach life in different ways, resulting in variation in the ways women and men *tend to* do things, including leadership. Thus, regardless of whether gender is socially learned or biologically determined, Gipson et al. (2017), for example, finds in their meta-analysis of research of the last 30 years that women have been found across studies to apply greater degrees of empathy and better communication skills and participative approaches to leadership than men. Ironically, though, this suggests an *advantage* for women leaders. As noted through-out this book, and particularly in Chapters 3 and 4, modern leadership theory and practice acknowledge the value of developing people, making transformational and relational approaches particularly useful. In turn, there is a move away from directive methods and approaches to leadership that demand uncritical compliance. As noted, these older notions about leadership – while they still have their place in some spe-cific circumstances – are generally considered limited if organisations are to progress. Instead, organisations that invest in developing engagement amongst people are most likely to enable the value-adding inputs of knowledge, initiative, enthusiasm and gen-eral distribution of participation. In most cultures, the enactment and presentation of these people-centred approaches tend to be associated with the feminine category rather than the masculine one, though.

In most cultures, the nurturing, negotiation, communication, concern for people skills, etc., are associated with idealised images of women, while confidence, directive, competitive and assertive skills are associated with idealised images of men. Much of this is crystallised in Alice Eagly's theorising of social roles. Introduced in the 1980s and updated in 2012, Eagly explains that the characteristics attributed as masculine or femi-nine are rooted in culturally informed expectations and therefore are *stereotypes* rather than actual properties of exclusively men or women (Eagly, 1987; Eagly and Wood, 2012). In a recent paper, Eagly and colleagues show how cultural norms of women have evolved over the last century in the USA. This observation of change lends support to the argu-ment that gender-based idealisations are socially constructed and context bound rather than natural or fixed; if they were determined and natural they would not change in a couple of generations (Eagly et al., 2020). Certainly, once reflected on, the attribution of masculine and feminine seems pretty unreliable. For example, it would be as unreason-able to assume that a man will not exhibit compassion as it would be to assume that a woman will not be competitive. Indeed, little consistent correlation of any specific attrib-ute with either men or women has been found across studies (Ferrer-Pérez and Bosch-Fiol in 2014 is just one example) – an item ostensibly feminine may readily be exhibited by men, and vice versa. Regardless, though, at a societal level, expectations of social behaviour are gendered, whereby men and women are stereotyped and idealised in different ways in virtually all cultures in the world.

If the sorts of skills and behaviours that are best for developing people in organisation are the collaborative, communications and negotiation ones, though, then the suggestion is that women will be *more*, not less, effective leaders than men. Indeed, at a broad level, these highly effective techniques, tendencies and approaches to leading have been reported in academic work (e.g. Jin, 2010 and Nassar et al., 2021), and amongst practitioners, including the leadership development consultant specialists Jack Zenger and Joseph Folkman (e.g. Zenger and Folkman, 2019). In these and other studies the observation is that these are characteristic of the ways *women* are likely to approach leadership. However, the fact remains that women are substantially *less* likely to be in leadership roles in organisations than men. The sections that follow explore the data that relates to this and some of the reasons why this might be the case.

WOMEN AND LEADERSHIP

No matter where you are in the world and what the socio-historical trajectory of gender equality looks like, women are under-represented in leadership roles. Despite gender equality featuring as a key part of their Sustainable Development Goals (SDGs), the UN reported in 2021 that across countries only 21 per cent of government ministers are women, and women make up only a quarter of the members of national parliaments. Of course there is some considerable variation by country: only four countries in the world have no female government representation at all, and at the other end of the scale, only four countries have equal to or greater representation of women compared to men (these are Rwanda, Cuba, Bolivia and the UAE) (UN Women, 2021). The more common under-representation of women leaders in public office is replicated in organisations, whereby even in countries with legislative equality between men and women in terms of rights and access to opportunity, there are substantially fewer women in leadership roles. The annual *Women in Business Report* by Grant Thornton, one of the world's biggest professional services networks, finds that throughout the world, as of 2021, women represent less than a third of the business leaders. Within this, Africa and South and East Asia show the highest rates of women leaders, with North America and Asia Pacific countries lower (Grant Thornton, 2021). This demonstrates that the time and extent of legislative gender equality in a nation is not necessarily a reliable indicator of the extent to which women will be observable in

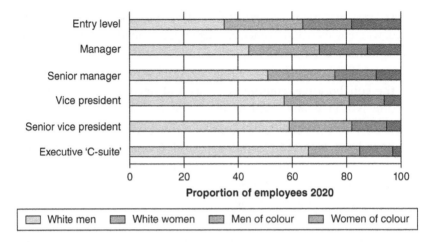

Figure 6.1   Pipeline of employees in corporate USA by race and gender

Source: McKinsey & Co and LeanIn (2020).

leadership positions. For several years the global management consultancy McKinsey & Co. has worked together with LeanIn, the women's network inspired by Facebook chief operating officer Sheryl Sandberg to produce its Women in the Workplace Report on the diversity of business leaders in the USA. Using data from 2020, Figure 6.1 illustrates that on entry to the job market, men and women are represented in pretty equal measure. Thereafter, the proportion of women falls at each subsequent level. The data shows that while this is true for all women, it is most marked for women of colour in the USA.

In summary, therefore, no matter the country, women tend to be under-represented in leadership roles in organisations compared with men. The following sections explore some of the potential reasons why this might be the case.

EXPLAINING LOW RATES OF LEADERSHIP AMONGST WOMEN

Since leadership effectiveness between men and women does not vary, and the collaborative, person-centred approaches to leading that are particularly suitable for modern organisations are in fact most commonly associated with women, it seems counter-intuitive that rates of leadership amongst women – at least as suggested by headship roles – are markedly low. This section explores this apparent anomaly via three key pillars: *ability, perceptions of ability* and *cultural expectations and discrimination.*

Ability

In some countries girls do not have the same access to education as boys, although the United Nations Educational, Scientific and Cultural Organization reports that these figures are improving (UNESCO, 2020). Even in countries where access to education is equal, however, types of education still vary considerably between girls and boys. This variation in education informs ongoing skills and human capital and this is likely to affect what people can do in their lives, especially their working lives. It also undoubtedly has an effect on rates of leadership. For example, in the UK, where there has been equal access to education for more than a century, the Higher Education Statistics Agency (HESA) reports that more than half of university students are female (around 56 per cent); however, there is significant variation in subjects studied by gender. Figure 6.2 illustrates that in the UK there are higher proportions of women studying medical and social subjects and higher proportions of men in science, technology and construction.

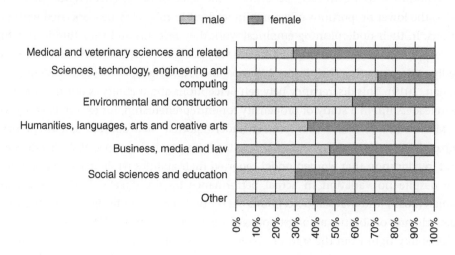

Figure 6.2   Subjects studied at university by gender in the UK
Source: HESA (2021).

When distribution of education, such as that illustrated in Figure 6.2, transfers into the workforce it creates greater proportions of men in engineering and technology industries, representing much of the private corporate world, and greater proportions of women in social and medical services industries, with less representation in corporations. In addition, the industries predominated by men tend to be those with higher financial value and overall economic power, compared to the industries that are predominated by women. These are all generalisations of course, but at a statistical level, they place men as more likely to be in economically powerful industries and women in caring or social ones. It also goes some way to explaining why there are more men than women in corporate leadership positions – they tend to be qualified in corporate-type industries in greater proportions than women. What this does not explain, though, is why the distribution of leaders remains unequal outside of the corporate domain. If women are over-represented in social, educational and medical work, why are they still under-represented in leadership roles in these sectors? Again, there may be several reasons, but given that this section has shown that levels of ability and human capital are, for the most part, reasonably consistent between men and women, let's turn first to *perceptions* of ability.

Perceptions of ability

As noted earlier, the leadership consultants Zenger and Folkman report the tendency for leadership practice amongst women to be consultative and person-centred. Consequently, they hypothesise that if women leaders have the same or better effectiveness than male leaders, the lower proportions of women in leadership roles may be associated with perceptions. In their underpinning empirical work they test this and they find in fact that self-perceptions about leadership abilities do vary between men and women, with women broadly under-reporting their leadership capabilities and men over-reporting (Zenger and Folkman, 2019). This discrepancy between perceptions about ability is not new or exclusive to leadership. In a study of propensity for entrepreneurship, for example, Langowitz and Minniti (2007) found that females under-reported their abilities as entrepreneurs compared with men, and ten years before that the psychology specialist Claude Steele found in education that women under-reported their abilities while males over-reported them despite no variation in actual performance by sex (Steele, 1997). Zenger and Folkman (2019) find that self-perceptions of ability to lead varies by age too, with greatest underestimates of abilities amongst younger women (those under 25). This underestimation of ability right from the start of careers is one potential reason why women may be less likely to go for leadership roles. The perceptions of others are also influential, though, and these are informed in large part by the prevailing socio-cultural environment. It is to cultural expectations of women and the potential influence of this on leadership that we turn next.

Cultural expectations and discrimination

In all countries, regardless of socio-historical trajectory or formal structural environment, women are more often than men responsible for the management and maintenance of domestic life. This may include responsibility over food preparation and accommodation, and overwhelmingly refers to care for children and other family. The economic geographers Katherine Gibson and Julie Graham refer to this as unpaid labour. They maintain that while traditional methods of exploring economic life account only for waged labour, in fact unpaid domestic work is one of the most substantial contributors to the socio-economic landscape in most countries (Gibson-Graham, 2008). Indeed, in the UK alone, journalist Jasmine Andersson reports in an article in 2020 that the value of this work is around £700 billion per annum.

The issue this creates in careers is that if women are bearing the greater share of domestic responsibility and work, regardless of structure and legislation in a country, the time and energy to invest in career building is diminished. As the employment scholar Greg Hundley puts it, 'individuals have finite stocks of human energy' (Hundley, 2000, p. 97). But this is an issue that lies at the surface of a deeper set of inequalities that are experienced throughout the lives of women compared with men. There is argument that the division of responsibility for domestic life is natural and there is argument that it is imposed. Again, this debate will rage on. Alice Eagly and Wendy Wood provide a useful summary of the nature–nurture debate over the last few decades (Eagly and Wood, 2013). For our purposes here it is largely irrelevant, though. The fact is that whether imposed or natural, or a bit of both, within the family structures of almost all cultures in the world, since women bear more of the burden for domestic life than men, there has evolved a cultural expectation that they will (or should) be prioritising family over work. At the same time of course, in many cultures there is the equally contentious notion that men will (or should) be prioritising work over family. These issues have been challenged, debated and legislated (for and against greater equality) for centuries. For leadership specifically, though, gender-based social and cultural expectations and ways of life inform how we think about leadership; there are still prevailing notional ideas about what leadership is and what leadership looks like – the *implicit leadership theories*. Most often in most countries, it tends not to look like a woman.

Thus, despite the convergence of stereotypically female-type skills being associated with effective modern leadership approaches and outcomes, the lingering expectation in most cultures in the world is that women are less likely to be leaders. Certainly, there have been and continue to be some spectacular and high-profile examples of female leaders, but the reality for many women in careers has been that obtaining leadership roles can be challenging in terms of both having sufficient time and energy, and fitting with the expectations of the prevailing socio-culture.

Of course, this continues to evolve. Decades of role models and modern styles of leading all inform social culture and women themselves about the potentials and approaches to leading that women may adopt. In particular, and possibly accelerated by the Covid-19 pandemic, the role of emotional intelligence has been a topic of much debate. Proposed in the 1990s by Daniel Goleman, emotional intelligence is described as comprising *self-awareness, self-regulation, passion, empathy* and *social skills* (Goleman, 1998a, 1998b, 2000). Conceptualisations of emotional intelligence have since been refined, and it has received much research attention as a key feature of working relationships in countless studies of organisations and leaders, synthesised somewhat in a meta-analysis by O'Boyle et al. (2010). This goes hand in hand with other emerging ideas about what leading should involve, with greater focus on social and ethical behaviours and empathy emerging in the last two decades (see Chapter 8 for more on ethics and leadership). It was New Zealand Prime Minister Jacinda Ardern who famously crystallised this *thought leadership* when she told the *New York Times*, 'One of the criticisms I've faced over the years is that I'm not aggressive enough or assertive enough or maybe somehow, because I'm empathetic, it means I'm weak … I refuse to believe that you cannot be both compassionate and strong' (Dowd, 2018). It remains to be seen whether these new ways of perceiving what leadership is and what it is for and how it may be enacted evolve.

For now, though, in summary, there is a complex and overlapping set of issues that affect women's ability to access leadership roles. Cultural expectations may lead to women selecting themselves out of leadership roles at greater rates than men do, or they may lend themselves to discriminatory practices whereby either consciously or unconsciously women are not considered for leadership positions in organisations in the same proportions as men. Critical to either of these reasons is authenticity. As noted in earlier chapters throughout this book, trust is a critical element in the practice of leading people. Research has identified that followers put trust above all other factors in determining good leadership, and much of the modern thinking about leadership, especially transformational and relational approaches, has trust front and centre as essential. Trust requires authenticity – you cannot trust someone you do not believe is presenting a true impression of themselves. Research has found that this authenticity is an issue especially pertinent for women leaders, as explained in Box 6.1.

Box 6.1: Authenticity, female leadership and imposter syndrome

In a seminal paper in 2005, Alice Eagly proposed that because of our traditional social ideas of what leadership looks like, it is more challenging for women than men to be identified as a leader (and this is as true for any group that has had limited access to leadership roles). In this sense, we turn once again to *implicit leadership theories* and *leadership concepts* and how they can serve to disadvantage those who do not fit notional ideas about leaders. For women, specifically, there can be a particular mismatch in terms of authenticity (Eagly, 2005). If cultural expectations of women valorise things like compassion, caring and passivity, but cultural expectations of leaders valorise things like authority, independence and competitiveness (the same things as for men generally), there exists a tension for women. As a member of a social culture, the challenge is the balance between identification with and presentation of identity as a 'good woman' and identification and presentation as a 'good leader'. Informed by Butler's theorising, this positions leadership as *performative*: we perform leadership within expectations (Butler, 1990). That being the case, a mismatch between expectations of idealised women and idealised leaders can lead to the phenomenon of 'imposter syndrome' for some women. Medical scholars Mullangi and Jagsi (2019) define imposter syndrome as self-doubt regardless of capability. It points to the tension between authenticity (in this case, as a woman) and authenticity as a leader, a tension that has to be managed. Of course, it would be a generalisation to say that it has to be managed by only women; men comply with the implicit leadership theories of society and organisations too, but for men there is a better match between idealised masculine behaviours and most versions of *implicit leadership theory*.

A review of the autobiographies of high-profile leaders such as the former Australian Prime Minister Julia Gillard and the USA's former Secretary of State Hillary Clinton in Kapasi et al. (2016) illuminates how these famous women have managed the authenticity challenge. Further, along with colleagues, I conducted and reported research on authenticity as a leader amongst entrepreneurs. Similar to findings about leadership in other domains, while the tension between stereotypes prevails – in this case stereotypes relating to women, leaders *and* entrepreneurs – optimal techniques for entrepreneurship again resonate with stereotypically *female* behaviours; entrepreneurs rely heavily on relational and transformational approaches that communicate vision, personalise the mission and bring people in on the development and realisation of an entrepreneurial start-up. As such, the consistently observed low rates of women entrepreneurs compared with men throughout the world is most accurately attributed to structural and cultural contexts rather than any deficit in ability or performance (Galloway et al., 2015).

PERSPECTIVES FROM PRACTICE 6.1

Perceptions and diversity

Claire McCarthy is the Director of Operations and HR at a large children's charity in Wales. More information about Claire can be found on page 2.

Victor Ikande is a regional head for the US-based construction firm Hollins. More information about Victor can be found on page 3.

Claire McCarthy relates her experience of being a woman leader in the UK charity sector, and especially when she had children. She notes:

(Continued)

I was 30 when I had a baby. I was in a middle-management position but had a UK-wide remit. At that time, you went out of the workforce, there was no option for the man to take leave, so you went out on your maternity leave. But when you came back there was a real sense among me and other women that you had to really give it your all when you came back, you know. You couldn't be late for work. You couldn't not stay – if you're sitting at five o'clock in a meeting that was going beyond your time and you've got to pick up from the nursery and your heart would be pounding out of your chest because you really were afraid to say, 'I'm going to have to go'. It was only actually when I was in a meeting and a man got up at five o'clock and said, 'Well, I need to go and get the kids now'. And it was almost like that parting the clouds moment where I thought, 'Why do I feel that I can't say that? What am I so ashamed of?'. That is changing now, though, because certainly where I am now there is a lot more acceptance of the fact that it is actually OK to have children. No one's going to think any the worse of you.

This heightened feeling of having to be irreproachable at work is echoed by Victor Ikande. He describes his experience of what it was like to work in the construction sector as an ethnic minority in the UK, having been brought up in Nigeria. He recalls some of the attitudes he encountered earlier in his career:

Construction is not the nicest place to start with. I mean you meet all sorts on a construction site, right? And so it's about getting the benefit of the doubt, if you know what I mean: this Nigerian guy rocks up and he's about to tell your foreman what to do. Do you take him seriously? No, not instantly, of course not. And that was always a barrier. I never got that benefit of the doubt instantly. Even at the office level I didn't get that. You don't inspire confidence instantly. So you have to break that barrier over time. But what was more important at that time was the guy at the top showed that confidence and it infected the rest of the people eventually. Because they know that, yeah, if this guy has his ear and he trusts him then we can start trusting him too. That was quite key. But there were still huge barriers when he wasn't there. You don't get as much room for error, you almost have to be the best, you have to be almost faultless, because there's always less tolerance when you're someone from a different country. That was a challenge in the early part of my career.

In terms of culture, Victor describes the construction sector as traditionally male and thus driven by a specific type of leadership. He explains:

It's an industry that has in the past just been driven by the worst kind of toxic masculinity. And it can be seen as strong leadership, right? So you can imagine what that means. For you to be more empathetic, you know it's just gonna be like, 'What is this?'. And leading by example, when you show yourself as a leader being that kind of person, then it leaks throughout the industry, if you know what I mean. The image is the rude person, he doesn't give a damn, he gets it done. And he is the person that is celebrated for the most part in this industry, and that makes it quite difficult.

Perspectives from practice questions

1. Why do you think both Victor and Claire report feeling like they have had to outperform other people at certain points in their careers?
2. Do you think it can be hard to lead people when you are an ethnic minority in the group?
3. Why do you think Victor describes the leadership concept in construction to be 'quite difficult'?

PERSPECTIVES FROM PRACTICE 6.2

Jannie Tam is the founder of the Hong Kong-based talent development company GROWDynamics. More information about Jannie can be found on page 1.

Priyanka Thali is a managing editor at CACTUS Communications, a technology company headquartered in India. More information about Priyanka can be found on page 3.

The three women leaders profiled in this book, Jannie Tam, Claire McCarthy and Priyanka Thali, each have different views on being a woman and a leader.

Claire McCarthy

Claire's testimony suggests some female traits can act to disadvantage, but also identifies assets such as attention to detail, humility and empathy:

> There's obviously different types of women, but I would say that I'm probably disadvantaged by a lot of female traits. I've got a soft voice, I don't shout. I work in a sector where quite often something that we're working on is emotionally moving, or emotionally disturbing. When I worked in the global aid charity it could be about mass famine ... These are upsetting things, these are human beings. Sometimes I think that can be wrongly perceived as you being weak if you're emotionally upset or emotionally moved by an experience of another human being. But it is not a weakness, it's empathy.
>
> I think also that there are much bigger issues, societal issues with unconscious bias. I think the language women use at the boardroom table

(Continued)

is slightly different to the language that the men use. For example, the woman at the table will say, 'I think we need to look into that. I'm not sure that's 100 per cent accurate', but the man will say, 'That's wrong'. Women tend to hedge their bets, men have the confidence; whether they actually have the evidence to have that confidence or not ... but nonetheless they have it. I have also noticed that whether they mean to or not, men will listen to other men maybe a wee bit more, give maybe a wee bit more gravitas to what a man is saying than what a women is saying and again it's maybe just based on that kind of very nuanced language that women tend to use, which I am positive is derived from a lack of confidence generally speaking, where they don't want to commit 100 per cent: 'Listen I'm pretty sure I'm right but let me check', whereas, like I say, the men are more bombastic and they'll just say, 'That's wrong' or 'That's right' or 'This is the way it is'.

I don't know which approach works best, though. I do think that I've seen much more backlash from staff to women bosses. I think there's a higher expectation of women in the workplace in leadership. I think there is an expectation that we will be more collaborative. I don't know how conscious people are of that bias but do I think that. And I do too! I think when I've got a woman boss, I actually expect her to be somewhat more considerate than a man boss. So I think that women start off a little bit disadvantaged but at the same time for me it works as an advantage because I am more collaborative and I am more considerate because that's what people expect me to be. The bad side is I'm more sensitive. So when they challenge me I do find it hurtful. I do think if I was a 50-year-old man would you be questioning me. Men I've worked with don't seem to be challenged in the same way as women and maybe it's because women invite the challenge. Because I will say, 'I want your opinion, I want to know how you feel about this, I want you to tell me if I've missed something', whereas men seem to be a bit more dictatorial. Sometimes I think my life would be easier if I took a male approach, but I can't because it's not who I am. I think that I expect to be challenged as a collaborative and female leader. I don't know if men expect the same challenge. But it can be an advantage because if women do have to evidence a little bit more why they think something is a good idea then they're ready to justify it, and I think that can work really well because I think it shows that you've thought about your idea and there's a depth to it. I've walked away from ideas that a man has had, when I've questioned the validity and they haven't had an answer. I've walked away with a wee bit of a lack respect, thinking you just want to stick a big plaster on this problem, you've not thought about the problem it's going to give us in six months' time.

Jannie Tam

Jannie feels that she leads in a way that is informed by being a woman:

> In Hong Kong, my experience as a woman leader has not been bad. I have been accepted. I didn't really experience unequal treatment. But I think generally people might feel like women can only do certain things. There are more guys out there and especially in technology, so it's always easier [for men] to get investment and there are less women doing this. But I would say even in a technology setting, women are important. The reason is because we are more empathetic. Empathy is the key thing nowadays. Everything is about empathy and leadership. Women are a lot more caring, a lot more empathetic and can look a lot more into human needs. And that gives a really good balance in the board level. I personally don't feel like it is important or necessary to fight to do all things like men. We should focus on what we're good at and try to amplify what we're good at, which is more of a human touch. We can be more empathetic, we can build relationships a lot easier with more levels of colleagues. So I think for me it is important to focus on what we as women can do. I'm not gonna fight with men. Me as a woman, I'm good at this and I'm gonna show you. But what I'm good at is equally important, if not more. I would say the highest level of leadership is to be able to connect with people, which women are very capable of doing.

Priyanka Thali

In terms of leading people, Priyanka has found CACTUS to be a good place to develop as a woman leader and she feels very supported, but she also notes that her experience may be anomalous in the wider Indian cultural milieu:

> Many people still see women having careers as something they do on the side and their primary role is to be a homemaker. I think that is something that is slowly changing, but it's still there and I have seen some of my friends experience that. You know, nobody asks men, 'So what are you going to do once you have a child, how are you going to do your job?'. But that's a question women still get asked ... I do have friends who have these difficulties in just being heard and in advancing and being considered for promotions or job opportunities because they're women or they're women with kids. It's the whole glass ceiling thing. I think it is there in most cultures. Women have all these responsibilities, so how will they manage things at work? But nobody questions that of a man who is married with kids, right?

(Continued)

Prikanka goes on to note that her awareness of these inequalities informs her leadership:

> I work with women with kids and I do see the struggles there. I do see how they try to balance their work as well their child-care responsibilities. I used to try to be understanding if on the work front things weren't going how they should be and I would think it's OK because I know that this person is having a tough time. But in the last few years I've tried to change that approach, so it's not about making allowances, it's about how to make that person perform at their best, despite having all of those responsibilities. So it's about how you can perform well irrespective, and trying to support that person and help them perform well even though they have these other things. So when my team members thought, 'OK, my manager understands that I have all this going on, so my manager is OK with me performing to this level', well, that became a problem and that is why I felt that things had to change. They may need support and the support I provide is mainly listening and giving them guidance about how to plan their day, how to manage their goals. And not sugar-coating it. The team member should know that I still have the same kinds of expectations from them as I have for my other team members who maybe don't have those responsibilities, but I can help them get support and give them visibility of that support. Many people don't realise that help can be provided, so it's about making that clear and visible.

Perspectives from practice questions

1. What do you think are the advantages and disadvantages Claire describes of her experiences of being a woman leader?
2. Do you think empathy is a weakness or an advantage in leadership?
3. Do you think there is a difference in the language male and female leaders use, as Claire suggests, in your organisation or industry?
4. Why can't Claire just adopt what she calls 'a male approach'?
5. Do you agree with Jannie that women are more empathetic and people-oriented than men? Is this true in your experiences of life, work, industry?
6. What are the advantages Jannie claims of having both men and women on boards?
7. Why do you think Priyanka has switched from excusing lower performance amongst women with dual work and life responsibilities to a more supportive position?
8. What might Priyanka do to support these colleagues?

DIVERSITY AND OUTCOMES, THE MORAL AND BUSINESSES CASES

This chapter has explored some of the issues associated with women and leadership, and women are deliberately profiled since they are universally under-represented in leadership roles in organisations. Other groups in different locations around the world suffer similar challenges and disadvantages when it comes to leadership of course. This section explores the implications of this for organisations and the leaders who might contribute in them. First, if we accept that inequality of opportunity is not fair, a moral case for greater equality is implied.

The moral case

The UN's Sustainable Development Goals (see Chapter 1) include specifically the aim of reducing gender inequality (SDG 5), but they include also an aspiration for reduced inequalities generally (SDG 10). One of the underpinning rationales for the prioritisation of reducing inequality is that equality of treatment and opportunity is identified as a human right (UN Sustainable Development Group, 2021). Along with other philosophical, humanistic and religious analysis, this thus underpins the *moral* obligation to commit to equality as a principle.

Alongside the moral case, there is the more pragmatic argument that if leaders are only drawn from a restricted pool of people, organisations (and societies) will miss out on the wider range of talents and skills. This is one of the main underpinnings of what is expressed next as *the business case*.

The business case

The business case for improving the proportions of leaders from diverse backgrounds includes that a greater amount of talent is available. This includes not just the inclusion of education and skills, but also the tacit knowledge they may bring, built from diverse experiences and lives. If organisations have leaders (or heads) who have broadly similar backgrounds, experiences and styles, then what may occur is just a revolving endorsement of the same sorts of ideas – a group-think scenario. Including individuals in leadership positions who have different backgrounds and experiences immediately introduces the potential for new ideas and new ways of doing things. It expands the knowledge in the decision-making leadership arenas. This is not a new idea. Throughout business studies it is well known that the greater the variety of sources of information, the greater is the range of opportunities that will emerge (e.g. Florida, 2003). Indeed, it has been long known that diverse and multiple sources of information are key enablers of ideas and innovation; this is the basic premise of Michael Porter's cluster theory (Porter, 1990). Followed through to the board level, there is a logical extrapolation that the more diverse the board, the richer the pool of information and knowledge available for ideas and decision-making. Put simply, a limited pool of people have only a limited range of knowledge to draw on. Diverse pools in comparison have diverse knowledge, experiences and perspectives and this informs decision-making. Take, for example, the scenario in Box 6.2.

Box 6.2: The value of diversity

A young tech start-up has two founders. They are new engineering graduates; each is male and aged 24. They have invented a device that improves safety from impact injuries to leg and foot joints. The idea is born of their mutual love of athletics and their engineering expertise. They imagine their main market is professional athletes. Directed by the bank as a condition of funding the founders are compelled to increase the range of knowledge on their board. As a result they take on two further directors. The first is a man aged 40 with a background in sales. He has two children aged 9 and 11. The other is a classmate from their university days, a woman aged 24 too, and like them, at the start of her career journey.

Immediately the two new directors inject new, valuable knowledge. The salesman proposes at their first meeting that the main market may not be professional athletes and the board might also consider parents of children. He reasons that since it is parents who will spend most often and in high amounts for a product like this they are an obvious choice. The new woman suggests also that there is actually a range of potentials for the technology, including dance and other sports such as gymnastics.

The original founders had not considered the potential of the mass children's market. Why would they? With no children, they had no notion of the scale of sports education for children, nor the depth of concern parents feel about injury. As devoted athletics enthusiasts, they also had not considered the potential for their innovation beyond athletics. The new, older man and the new woman on the board had brought with them not only their skills and enthusiasm, but their reflexive experiences and tacit knowledge about the world. These varied from the founder's experience and perspectives and this informed and added value to the whole business proposition.

While Box 6.2 presents a simplified example, it does illustrate that diversity is value-adding. This is evidenced in research studies in organisations, where the inclusion of women leaders has had a positive effect on performance. An example is a study by Joy et al. (2007), which shows better performance in terms of returns on equity, sales and invested capital in Fortune 500 companies that have women on their boards. It would be oversimplified to state that diverse boards are a silver bullet, though. Recent work by scholars such as Simionescu et al. (2021) show that there may not be improvement consistent across different measures (they find no effect on return on assets, for example). In addition, in their international meta-analysis of 140 studies, Post and Byron (2015) find variation depending on socio-cultural context; however, they also find that the inclusion of women on boards is consistently advantageous for strategy formation and governance.

PERSPECTIVES FROM PRACTICE 6.3

John Black is a station manager with one of the UK's fire and rescue services. More information about John can be found on page 2.

Interestingly, the two participant leaders in this book who work in traditionally predominantly male contexts were both very clear about the value they perceived of improving diversity, and especially the gender balance, in their sectors. First, in the fire service, John Black recalls a specific strategy to increase diversity:

All the changes came about the same time where we most definitely encouraged diversity within the fire service whether that be sexuality, religion or colour and creed, it all happened about the same time. So we had women coming into the fire service, ethnic minorities coming into the fire service. So it was very noticeable in the fire service when it first started, when the first female firefighter came in was very noticeable, when the first person of colour that came in very noticeable and, certainly in my experience, it was very welcomed because their influences made us realise that actually we need to change and so we made efforts to positively change.

We were finding it difficult to integrate into the community, in terms of being a group of all-male firefighters. For example, we sometimes found it difficult dealing with some of the new minorities particularly when there was an influx of migrants, and we didn't know the cultures, we didn't know how to speak to them, we didn't know much about them at all. Their cultures were different and we had to be able to adapt to the different cultures and create ways of dealing with that if we were to achieve our community objectives and service. So the fire service was very good at developing diversity and it really helped. I was looking forward to working with different types of people. I actually thought that bringing in their opinions would be a good thing for the fire service and I looked forward to hearing what they had to say because we were very closed at one stage in my career, it was just the way it was.

And it most definitely did change things and we had to consider our thoughts, words and actions carefully for a long time. So, yes, I guess leadership strategies did change, but for the better for everybody, it was a welcome change. Obviously, there was resistance, but they were very much in the minority and they were a quiet minority at that, but it was there. But it was a good thing and it changed the fire service for the better in my opinion and continues to do so.

The US-headquartered multi-national firm that Victor Ikande works for is going through a diversity process now. He describes it thus:

(Continued)

In our organization as part of the corporate strategy, within two years we need the gender split to be 50:50. All the leaders are judged on that. I am a leader so I am judged on that. Some people think its tokenism, but I don't believe that it is. The way I see that is that I've been given the opportunity to expand my talent pool in terms of where I can reach out for talents for those operational roles. I think it's giving us more opportunities because it helps address our unconscious biases. There are challenges. I'm in the Middle East so there can be even more challenges because of the cultural dimensions associated with that. But it's been a very interesting journey for me. It amazes me that once you switch that consciousness and you actually watch what's happening with the women in your team at work, then it starts becoming very apparent to you the challenges they're facing. I mean there are examples of a woman saying something five minutes before, and me saying the exact same thing after, and everybody would say to me, 'Amazing idea Victor'. I actually watch it and note it mentally. Some people will just not listen if it comes out of a woman. Sometimes we need to have a directive style in this work, we need to make sure the team comes in line. But that is not gender specific, absolutely not. But when I do it, I'm a strong guy; if a woman does it she gets called names. But this new agenda is very heavily driven in my company now, and that's reluctantly changing. I mean to be honest with you, I still see people having off-the-record conversations like, 'Oh yes, I know we have to listen to women, but ...', and that kind of thing, right. It is there, we cannot deny it. And it becomes obvious why all these years we've had that challenge, that imbalance. It becomes obvious because even when a multi-billion dollar company like Hollins comes out and says, 'We must have balance in any leadership position and at all levels', the men, when they are in their comfort zone, when there are no women in the room, still express their real opinions. You still see that reluctance. They don't even realise they're doing it. So when you know that as a leader, then you know you need to make very active efforts to make sure that those kinds of things are gone. So when you see that kind of behaviour, you try and address it directly. That's my style, I actually go and talk to the person about it and say, 'You know what you did today, I don't think you would have done it to a man'. They might become a bit defensive. But that's fine.

I think that, there's no doubt about it, in this industry there is toxic masculinity and it is celebrated. And that lends itself towards automatically making it difficult for a woman to advance in this game. So 50:50 in the next two years is very ambitious. And we're all judged by it. And I still have to deliver a project, I'm not getting any slack on my delivery. But because I'm now forced to think of a wider talent pool than I would have done before it's an advantage actually. And plus, some of the average males who would have got the positions normally will not get them anymore because they're average and there's somebody that's better who's going to get it now. So the average people are not going to get through the net to the top now because the leaders are being forced to think wider. And I think it's been huge. It's been a good journey. This company is great for that, I have to be honest with you. We have a leader, a CEO, who is genuine, he means what he says and he's really driven the message: 'We know the talent is out there but our pool is too narrow at the moment. Open up that pool and get the talent.' I thought it would be hard, especially in the Middle East, but it turns out it's not. They've [women] just been side-lined. The universities have been telling us there's plenty of women, and even in the workplace, before all of this – not by design, but by sort of coincidence – some of the top people, the top performers happen to not be males.

Perspectives from practice questions

1. What have been the advantages of the policy to increase diversity in the UK fire service?
2. Do you think greater diversity amongst people who work in the fire service has implications for the ways in which it is led throughout the hierarchy?
3. Why do you think the construction firm Victor works for has a target of a 50:50 gender balance across levels?
4. How has this strategy informed Victor, including his leadership?

This chapter has explored diversity and leadership and presented a moral case and a business case for inclusion. In essence, this brings us back to considering the role of organisations and leaders within them by raising the following questions:

*   Is profit maximisation the only imperative for commercial companies?
*   What really is the role of leadership in organisations (commercial or otherwise)?

These and other questions that relate to what organisations are for are discussed further in Chapter 8 on ethics and leadership. For now, the central points regarding gender and leadership are summarised below.

At its simplest:

There are notions about the differences between males and females in most cultures. At best, these are stereotypes, though.

Research finds no variation in leadership effectiveness between men and women.

Research finds some variation between men and women in terms of approaches to leadership, with stereotypical ideas about women presenting a greater fit with relational and transformational approaches.

Despite this, there may be a mismatch between the lifestyles of women with leadership roles compared with men, and there may be a mismatch between the cultural expectations of a good leader and a good woman.

It remains a fact that women are in leadership positions in organisations in much lower proportions than men.

There is evidence that diversity – in this case women – on boards is good for organisational performance because it breaks the group-think and communal endorsement of restricted decision-making and injects diversity of knowledge and ideas.

SUMMARY

This chapter has explored some of the key issues associated with leadership and diversity. It has largely focused on gender as an example of clear variation in rates of leadership consistent across the world. Many of the issues associated with gender and leadership resonate with other categories of diversity too, and the testimonies of some of the leaders profiled in this book attest to that.

Pertinently, in organisations in virtually all countries diversity is an issue. It seems counterintuitive, however, since organisations have so much to gain. Research has demonstrated in countless ways and across industries and sectors the value of diverse workforces and leadership. For organisations that seek to add value, the messages are clear, and yet men, and especially men of a country's predominant ethnicity, are still disproportionately represented in leadership positions. The fact that this is most marked in the private sector is the most perplexing of all. In the corporate world it is often asserted that only rational economics is at play and so structures and strategies dispassionately adopt the most effective business models. Perhaps there is as much idealisation of business culture as there is of the practices of different types of people.

EXERCISES

Consider the leadership concept in your organisation. Is it gendered?

Is there a type of person who is best suited to leading in your organisation?

Other than gender, what other types of inequality do you think affect the leadership rates in your organisation? Is this consistent throughout your industry or sector or country?

Are there barriers to women's advancement in your organisation or industry? What do you consider these barriers are?

Can people who are balancing career and domestic responsibilities become leaders?

How would you support the careers of people who are balancing work and substantial domestic roles:

- in your organisation?
- more generally in society?

Summarise some of the key reasons why women are less likely to be in leadership positions than men.

Give an explanation of the value of diversity on boards of directors.

Consider the socio-culture you live in. What are the conditions for having diverse leadership in organisations?

Give an explanation of why the approaches of women leaders may be well suited to modern organisations.

Give an explanation of imposter syndrome and explain how it affects the potential and practice for leadership.

7
LEADING AND CULTURE

The world has been becoming increasingly connected over a long period of time. Digital communications have enhanced the abilities to exchange ideas and knowledge and to trade in ways that were inconceivable in the past. While the technology to enable this interconnectedness has been developing for several decades, the Covid-19 pandemic compelled organisations and individuals to engage with these technologies and, at least for a time, these were the underpinning of sustainability of many organisations and resilience in the global crisis.

More generally, for many organisations, the interconnected world has produced all sorts of opportunities. Access to new markets has seen the transference of goods and services between regions and has enabled people from all over the world to work together. With this interconnectedness comes challenges too, though. There are different expectations, experiences and values expressed by people throughout the world. For organisations that trade with, or locate in, regions that diverge from their origins, there can be specific implications for leaders. This chapter explores some of these.

CROSS-CULTURAL AWARENESS

The term 'culture' may be explained as the collective customs, behaviours and values of a particular society. According to the *Oxford English Dictionary*, culture may be 'the customs and civilisation of a particular time' too. In this sense, culture may be understood as varying geographically throughout the world, and temporally whereby there can be generational cultural variation.

There are extensive bodies of knowledge about cultures – regional, national and organisational – throughout the sociology, ethnography, history and organisational behaviour literatures. In this chapter, we are less concerned with the various models of the roots, expression and development of cultures, and more focused on exploring the implications for leaders when they are engaged in organisational work that spans different cultures.

If we return to our distinction between *thought leadership* and *leading people* (see Chapter 1), there are different but overlapping issues. First, in terms of *thought leadership*, knowledge and experience of other cultures – or *cross-cultural awareness* – may prompt the generation of ideas and new opportunities. There is a long precedent of learning as a consequence of travel and communication outside of one's own cultural locale. Examples include commercial opportunities, such as the expansion of products and services into remote markets and the import of ideas, products and services from remote locations into local markets. Beyond the commercial world, there is also much exchange of ideas based on experience of different locations and their itinerant knowledge, traditions and customs, including different ways of doing things as diverse as constructing buildings, cooking food, educating children; the list is endless. As explored in Chapter 6, diversity is a breeding ground for new ideas, knowledge and development in humanity. Cross-cultural awareness can thus be instrumental in *thought leadership*.

The other key function of leadership, *leading people*, is also substantially affected by cross-cultural circumstances. There are two main ways in which leading people in cross-cultural circumstances plays out in organisational life. The first is where leadership is conducted in one location with people from different cultures, including diversity in terms of nationality or race, age-groups, or even work or topic traditions (it is plausible to consider the common customs and working practices of IT specialists, for example, or teachers, or artists as distinct cultures). The second type of cross-cultural scenario that has implications for leaders is in organisations that are spread geographically, such as multi-national enterprises (MNEs) or branch or franchise units in geographic locations remote from the headquarters. In either case – staff of different cultures in one location or geographically spread – there are serious implications for leaders. To influence people so as to extract the best effort from them, and in turn best support them to achieve, a leader must be cognizant and informed about the cross-cultural circumstances in which he or she is leading. This includes an awareness of the differences and nuances in experiences and expectations of leaders and of work amongst the different cultural groups throughout the organisation. What is advocated here is not merely a nod to inclusion, equality and harmonious relationships in organisations, though these are worthy ends in themselves. More pragmatically, it is only by understanding, at least in some wide sense, how people approach work, what they aspire to, what their expectations are, and how they relate to work and to the people (including the leadership) in organisations that a leader may engage meaningfully within that cultural context. In effect, then, cross-cultural awareness for leaders includes an appreciation of the diverse business, political and cultural environments of followers' experiences, and these may include:

- attitudes to work;
- working practices;
- social practices;
- ways of communicating;
- attitudes to and experiences of equality;
- expectations of work and careers;
- values.

Without cross-cultural awareness, a tension can emerge when the cultural experiences and expectations of those leading vary from those being led; more specifically, an apparent lack of fit of followers' behaviours with the expectations of leaders when those leaders have not taken account of cultural divergence can impinge on leadership ability, quality and effectiveness. For example, follower behaviour that is not congruent with leader expectations may be interpreted as a failing of some sort, perhaps a lack of engagement with the strategy or aims of the organisation, perhaps an unwillingness to work and contribute. In fact, it could be neither. It may merely signal ways of engaging with work and organisations that are culturally specific – and just not similar to 'head office' norms.

PERSPECTIVES FROM PRACTICE 7.1

Victor Ikande is a regional head for the US-based construction firm Hollins. More information about Victor can be found on page 3.

Jannie Tam is the founder of the Hong Kong-based talent development company GROWDynamics. More information about Jannie can be found on page 1.

Priyanka Thali is a managing editor at CACTUS Communications, a technology company headquartered in India. More information about Priyanka can be found on page 3.

Ken Lorenz is the owner of a data analytics firm and a data analytics consultancy, both based in the USA More information about Ken can be found on page 2.

Claire McCarthy is the Director of Operations and HR at a large children's charity in Wales. More information about Claire can be found on page 2.

In reflecting on being Nigerian, British and working in the diverse UAE context, Victor Ikande remarks:

> We are not as different as we think, believe it or not. We always thought that, right? Even growing up when I was at school and it was 99.9 per cent Nigerian people, it was my belief that I was different from British people. I thought I would never get along with anybody, you know. And then I came into

that country and came to realise that actually one's values get aligned and it's surprising how similar we all are. OK, there are situational adaptations, but in general I mean. It really surprised me. I'm sure that 22 years ago when I rocked up at Heathrow airport, I didn't think that you could ever form friendships with people from a different country. I just thought we are too different. Because if you think about if you are a little boy in Nigeria and you don't come across other people – all you see is the movies, right. And your perception of others is based on some movie that you've seen or on TV. So you're like, 'No way, what do I have in common with this'. And then you come into the country and you start building relationships and you find out that your values are more aligned than you had ever imagined. The Emirates is the same. But here there are people from everywhere, so it's more of a melting pot again.

Like Victor's experience in the UAE, Jannie Tam describes Hong Kong as highly diverse in terms of cultures:

Hong Kong is an international city so you have to engage with people from other markets. It's never just Hong Kong, it's Taiwan, it's got the Chinese touch, Western markets to deal with. So you have to be sensitive of people from different cultures. We have different customs and different priorities and different taboos that you have to avoid, right, but also at the same time you can see that people from all over the globe do also have some commonality. So try to focus on commonality and try to be sensitive about the differences. For example, Chinese people are relatively less vocal sometimes as compared with Western people.

Priyanka speaks similarly of India:

Coming from a country that is so diverse culturally and socially, I think that adapting to different cultures hasn't been such a challenge, because we have to do so much of that within our own country. We have people from the North who have a different way of communicating or working, and then we have people from the South who come from a different school of thought. Similarly from the East and the West. So I think adapting culturally is something that we are kind of used to doing. Whenever we work, we have to take cultural differences into account, religious differences into account, being able to respect that and live in harmony, and not just at the management level, but as a country. So I think for me personally, working with people from other parts of the world was just an extension of adapting to those cultural differences that I probably have already been brought up doing, respecting cultural diversity. Our client management department, they are client facing so they come from wherever

(Continued)

the largest markets are, so I have Japanese colleagues and Korean colleagues. I'm somewhat familiar with East Asian culture and how they communicate, how they expect requests to be made. I'm very conscious of that whenever I'm talking to them. I think being mindful is important, so how I'm positioning requests. And if I'm talking to somebody, say from India or maybe from the West, especially Americans, I know that they prefer direct communication, direct speech, so you know they don't want any roundabout talk. It's important to take all of those differences into account when you're communicating.

Ken Lorenz noted that when he developed his travel business in India, cultural practices did require a departure from his previous experiences of leading:

In India, they expected a strong leader, they respected a strong authoritarian leader in the workplace. And you had a clear hierarchy of people and penalties if people kind of got out of line seemed to be more important than rewards for constant good behaviour. Bonus structure motivated people, but punitive kept them in line. I took a lot of trips over there to meet people, to go work in the office for a couple weeks, and be hands-on with it to learn. But when I was trying to explain the kind of people we wanted [for the USA market-oriented business] it was much more difficult [to explain this] in India.

Priyanka Thali explains the traditional Indian culture and its expression in a modern and multicultural organisation thus:

India as a country, I guess, follows a largely directive style, and it's kind of interwoven into our culture and fabric that there is a 'higher up' and everybody listens to what that person has to say. So authoritarian, very directive, and that's how it's been in most corporate set-ups in India for the longest time. Of course, things are changing now, but that's how I was brought up and that's how I started out as a leader: people would have to more or less go with my decisions and I would be solely responsible for making the decisions. As a culture I think we place so much importance on work and getting the job done and not as much attention goes into a work–life balance and stress management and things like that as it should. But the Indian work culture in general is changing gradually of course ... For instance, managing Gen Z is fairly different from managing millennials and very different from managing Gen Y. And it's important to take those differences into account. In my experience of leading people who are who are slightly older, maybe either the baby-boomer generation or the Gen Y, things were very different for them, so in India they have grown up with the autocratic style or authority in style and they don't question authority. They don't believe that they might be doing something better, just whatever the manager says goes. Whereas with somebody who's

> Gen Z, I will see stuff being openly questioned. That may be a good thing or may not be a good thing, it depends on the situation in the context. But you see these varying differences and it's important that you understand where it's coming from. I think with the ones that are very compliant, you want them to be more empowered. You want them to be more independent thinkers, to come up with ideas or solutions on their own and letting them know that I will not always be right. You know, 'It's your call'. With the other side of the spectrum, the younger ones, I think, telling them 'You need to do this!' does not help at all. It does quite the opposite. So for them, I think, giving them that picture about, 'This will be the outcome if you don't do this. If you do this well, this is how it will benefit you'. So I think with the younger generation they need to have visibility on consequences.

Interestingly, Jannie in Hong Kong and Claire in the UK both reported similar variation in expectations amongst workers of different ages. The shift in culture over time underpins Jannie's business model in fact:

> GROWDynamics is basically about the style of learning. In my generation we grew up and basically learned by recall. We just got information, memorized everything and put it in the exam. So that's our upbringing educationally. But GROWDynamics is basically using a totally different style, to inspire critical thinking. So people don't just know something, they don't become a reporter of knowledge. They have to make sure that what they know makes sense to what they do. But in our genera-tion a lot of the leaders today they came from the learning background that is just compliance and listen and memorize. And we have to communicate with millen-nials and Gen Z, we have to understand this is their way of learning so we have to also equip ourselves, you know as an older generation of leaders talking to the younger ones. We have to bridge the mindset.

Claire's testimony mirrors this need to understand different generations:

> A lot of people that enter the workplace now are more confident and they live their lives differently to me. Young people have grown up in a digital age, as opposed to myself who didn't, and I think it plays out quite significantly in the workplace. Younger people feel much more entitled to have an opinion because they've grown up giving their opinion online and in public platforms. So I do feel a generational difference with that because I was never invited to give an opinion before I had any authority really. So there's a bit of a genera-tional issue going on, and I've found that can be a little challenging because I think they're being disrespectful and I've had to train myself that they're not being disrespectful, they're being confident and ambitious maybe. You know they're just voicing what they think and that's okay.

(Continued)

Perspectives from practice questions

1.   Jannie in Hong Kong, Victor in the UAE and Priyanka in Mumbai all note their cultural awareness because they work in highly diverse societies. When you reflect on your experience of work, how diverse is the context?
2.   Why do all the participants stress the need for cultural sensitivity as a leader?
3.   Why do you think what Ken wanted for his American business in terms of types of people was difficult to explain in India?
4.   Priyanka in India, Jannie in Hong Kong and Claire in the UK all remarked on the changing expectations and attitudes to work amongst younger people. Is this consistent with your experience in your organisation or industry or country?

As the testimonies above suggest, there are differences between people in different cultures. Acknowledgement of this is only part of the means by which leadership effectiveness in cross-cultural contexts can be optimised. Take Claire's story below, which relates an example where reliance on incomplete, anecdotal knowledge of a culture had a demotivating effect, ultimately detrimental to the organisation.

PERSPECTIVES FROM PRACTICE 7.2

Claire describes cultural issues in a previous organisation:

> When I worked in international aid that was intercultural because there were people from all over the world. That wasn't a problem. But there were a lot of inter-UK cultural issues. I lived in Glasgow at the time and we had an office in London, an office in Belfast, an office in Cardiff and the office in Glasgow. And I think it's fair to say that Cardiff, Belfast and Glasgow very much felt patronised by the London office. There was a general assumption always that our communities were poor and that we were parochial but there was never evidence to back that up. I would hear people in London have an idea about community fundraising, for example, and refer to Scotland as parochial, people who had never been there, that had never researched any data from there. And I remember having to, at quite a young age, challenge that and say, 'Well I live in a big multicultural city. I actually don't know who my neighbours are. I don't have a community hall that I attend'. But their assumption about other regions of the UK was that we all lived in a village and that we were poor and so wouldn't raise funds. I think most of us are gone from there now – just felt insulted and patronised so I moved on.

Claire's testimony illustrates how easy it is to assume we know a culture. Popular media and racial and national stereotypes have often exacerbated these misunderstandings. In fact, so too have some of the more formal means by which we have analysed culture in scholarship. The next section explores two major international studies that have had a huge influence on our understanding of leadership in cross-cultural contexts: Hofstede's cultural dimensions theory and the more recent GLOBE study.

STUDIES OF CULTURE AND LEADERSHIP

This section provides a summary of Hofstede's cultural dimensions theory and the GLOBE project. They are included here to showcase both as high-profile works of international research on cultural variation. They are not the only means by which scholars have engaged with culture, but they are both heavily referenced throughout business and leadership studies.

Hofstede's cultural dimensions

During the 1960s and 1970s, Geert Hofstede conducted surveys with staff who worked for the US-headquartered technology firm IBM in one of the 40 countries it operated in at that time (it currently operates in 171). Using data from these surveys, Hofstede developed *cultural dimensions theory* (Hofstede, 1980, 1991, 2001). Cultural dimensions theory proposes a set of 'dimensions' that vary between cultures and these are configured to capture and explain differences in social and behavioural practices throughout the world. Originally Hofstede proposed four dimensions: *power distance, individualism versus collectivism, uncertainty avoidance* and *masculine versus feminine* (Hofstede, 1980). Further surveys including more IBM territories followed, as did the input of other scholars such as Michael Bond and Michael Minkov, who extended the instrument to other companies and sectors (Hofstede and Bond, 1988; Minkov, 2011; Minkov and Hofstede, 2012). Consequently, a further two dimensions were added. These were *long- versus short-term orientation* and *indulgence versus restraint*. The six cultural dimensions are summarised in Table 7.1.

The information in Table 7.1 refers specifically to the six dimensions of culture as described by Hofstede and colleagues. The examples given refer to geographic locations. Two caveats therefore must be expressed. First, as noted already, culture refers to more than just regional variation and there have been studies that have explored Hofstede's dimensions by other cultural expressions (Hofstede, 2001, 2011). Second, the geographic examples given are at best sweeping generalisations. Therein lies one of the key criticisms of Hofstede's theory of cultural dimensions. These are summarised later in this chapter, but first we turn to another model of cultural dimensions that relates specifically to leadership: the GLOBE cultural dimensions.

Table 7.1   Hofstede's cultural dimensions

Dimension	Description	Examples
Power distance	Different attitudes to power between leaders and followers. High power distance describes inequality, remoteness and inaccessibility between leaders and followers.	High power distance is found in countries such as Malaysia and other places in Asia, and in Russia. Low power distance countries include some northern European ones, New Zealand and Australia.
Individualism or collectivism	The extent to which society prioritises the interests of the individual or the group. The extent to which people are seen as independent or as part of a collective.	The USA and some parts of Europe are individualistic cultures where life and work are the responsibility and duty of individuals to themselves. Sub-Saharan African nations, much of South Asia and some South American states have more collectivist cultures where responsibility and duty to the wider family or social group are prioritised.
Uncertainty avoidance	The extent to which uncertainty and ambiguity are tolerated within a culture; the extent to which people are comfortable with an unknown future.	Japan and Greece have been found to have high levels, suggesting a preference for planning and precedence. Scandinavian countries are said to have low uncertainty avoidance, suggesting they are comfortable with new ways of doing things.
Masculine or feminine cultures	The extent to which a culture expresses normative notions about masculinity, such as assertiveness and rewards, or normative notions about femininity, such as cooperation and compassion (but see Chapter 6 on these as stereotypes).	Japan, Italy and Austria are said to have high masculinity cultures, and Scandinavian countries and some South American ones have been described as high femininity.
Long-term orientation or short-term orientation	The extent to which tradition is valued over innovation and change. Long-term orientation describes a commitment to re-creation of social life, while short-term orientation describes an openness to change.	China and Japan are described in Hofstede and colleagues' works as long-term oriented, whereas USA and Canada are described as short-term oriented.
Indulgence or restraint	The extent to which leisure and enjoyment are enabled or constrained, whether that be formal via regulation or informal by social norms.	Many states in Western Europe are categorised as indulgent, whereas Eastern Europe and much of Asia are described as restraint cultures.

GLOBE

The Global Leadership and Organizational Behavior Effectiveness (GLOBE) project is an ongoing study of leadership and culture as expressed throughout the world. It was

Table 7.2 GLOBE cultural dimensions

Dimension	Description
Uncertainty avoidance	Extent to which people avoid uncertainty by adherence to norms and traditions
Power distance	Extent to which people expect power to be hierarchical and remote
Institutional collectivism	Extent to which organisations and society enable collective effort
In-group collectivism	Extent to which people feel loyalty and belonging
Gender egalitarianism	Extent to which gender equality is achieved
Assertiveness	Extent to which people are aggressive and confrontational
Future orientation	Extent to which people future plan and defer returns
Performance orientation	Extent to which people are rewarded for performance
Humane orientation	Extent to which people are rewarded for fairness and altruism

developed from Hosfstede's theory and there remain both operational and conceptual overlaps with Hofstede's model. Developed by Robert House in the 1990s, the GLOBE project focuses on leadership specifically and the effects of different cultures on it (House et al., 2001). As of 2020, it includes data from 62 countries, with a new expansion with a greater number of collaborators in process. There have been multiple publications over the years and spin-off research projects based on this massive data-gathering collaboration, including multi-country studies of leadership effectiveness amongst C-suite executives and throughout the range of leadership levels (House et al., 2004, 2013).

Broadly, the key premise supported by the GLOBE data is that leadership varies by social culture, including attitudes to leading and expectations of leaders. In the GLOBE study, the world is split into ten clusters, and based on responses to the GLOBE survey the cultures are compared via nine cultural dimensions, as per Table 7.2.

GLOBE suggests that there are approaches to leadership, or leadership styles, that are more or less appropriate based on the cultural norms and preferences in a region. Consequently, optimal leadership varies by culture, with, for example, participative and team-building approaches most appropriate in some regions because of the types of culture there. Rather than detail the mapping of these, for our purposes here it is sufficient to note that Hofstede and GLOBE both show that values, beliefs, ways of thinking and behaving vary across humanity, and for us the implication is that optimal leading will account for that.

At its simplest: Cultural dimensions theories propose that cultures vary across regions in distinct ways that can be measured.

Critique of cultural dimensions theories and their application to leadership

One of the key issues with the cultural dimensions theories is that they are by default generalisations of cultures, and at one point in time at that. As Jepson (2009) notes, neither nations nor cultures are static; instead at any point in time they are multiple, and they develop over time too. In addition, by grouping people regionally, categories are created and characteristics attributed according to the responses of people in these categories. But as McSweeney (2002) points out, humans are not easily categorised and there is enormous variation within categories. Consequently, cultural dimensions theories are a blunt interpretation of culture, and it is perfectly possible for individuals and even groups within a region to act in ways not congruent with the overall cultural category. Pertinent to this is inspection of attitudes and beliefs as they vary by demography within a region too – cultural dimensions theories do not deal well with variations by gender or age or other distinctions, but these distinctions may be significant in terms of implications for leadership.

Mirroring this problem of generalisation and lack of accounting for in-groups and other variations is that the regions defined in cultural dimensions theories are entirely constructed. Close inspection of culture when explored by region can show only broad patterns. It may be the case that the people who live in a region where national borders meet have more in common with each other than with each of their respective nations or regions defined along geo-political (or research) lines. Equally, many countries have pluralist populations, where may cultures co-exist, and different cultures prevail in alignment with some other antecedent, such as shared history or trauma or religion. Thus, just as the cultural norms and values of all people in a country are not consistent, neither are cultures clearly distinct from each other as defined by hard borders, a point noted in Monir Tayeb's and George Graen's critiques of Hoftede and GLOBE respectively (Tayeb, 2001; Graen, 2006).

Lastly, cultural dimensions theories have developed from evidence generated by Western-informed research studies. As a result, there is an argument that what they actually present is a Western interpretation of a social culture, elicited by having local people complete a survey that is inherently Western in design and structure. There is argument that unless you are embedded in a culture, it is not possible to understand it sufficiently well for comparison of the type to which cultural dimensions theories aspire. That being the case, cultural dimensions theories rely on cultural *stereotypes* according to scholars such as McCrae (2008), for example. Culture is described as richer than that, including variation demographically and temporally, and as such cultural dimensions theories have been charged with being limited in terms of what they can tell us about complex and nuanced cultures and their development for the purposes of informing knowledge (e.g. Venaik and Brewer, 2013 in marketing).

To summarise, therefore, cultural dimensions models have been criticised for being:

- generalisations;
- snapshots in time;
- unable to account for in-region variation based on demography or migration or political/historical variation;
- too reliant on geo-political borders and not equipped to deal with overlaps;
- Western-centric, thus presenting Western *interpretations* of global cultures.

Despite these, the Hofstede and GLOBE models do reveal differences between cultures at considerable scale, over a sustained period and in a replicable way. They have shown that variation exists and have spotlighted that the cultural values, experiences, expectations and sensitivities of people – even if they are generalised – are important. For leadership they are particularly pertinent in terms of affording some direction to matching leader approach to follower culture. These studies have created a platform from which knowledge and practice may develop and refine. New ways of measuring culture are always evolving in the academic literature. Examples of these include the application in leadership studies of Mary Douglas's cultural theory (Douglas, 1970), which explores different people's attitudes to risk (e.g. Salih, 2020), and the work of Earley and Ang (2003) on modelling cultural intelligence. In addition, and pertinent for our purposes here, in terms of practice there is much value to informing leaders of the importance of cognizance of and sensitivity to follower expectations and attitudes to work in organisations. These are the legacies of these scaled projects.

CROSS-CULTURAL LEADING IN PRACTICE IN ORGANISATIONS

Where there is cultural variation because of diversity within organisations, a one-size-fits-all approach to leading is unlikely to be successful. Alongside this, though, organisational leaders have to advocate and represent the organisation's core values. Leadership therefore involves the intellectual reasoning required to balance the interests and values of the organisation with those of the cultures from which stakeholders derive. This has implications for *thought leadership*. It also has particular implications for *leading people*. For optimal engagement with followers an informed and flexible approach to leading people must be taken, with some sensitivity for their experiences, expectations, attitudes to work and values. There is resonance here with context and situational approaches to leading. In all instances, information and knowledge will inform, so the better prepared a leader, the better their ability to lead cross-culturally. Associated with this, perhaps a leader may modify (within organisational culture parameters) their style and approach in line with the culture of followers or context.

Critically, if leaders of people are to engage followers effectively and extract optimal effort and excellence, then they must be cognizant of the different perspectives and tastes of other cultures. Whether referring to multi-national enterprises or to diverse organisations in a single location, leaders will also be more effective where they demonstrate respect for followers from a cultural perspective, rather than an absolute ethnocentric imposition of the 'head office' culture. The avoidance of implying that one culture is superior to another is a critical element in establishing the trust and communications and engagement associated with transformational and relational approaches to leading. This has never been more pertinent than now, with the ubiquity and development of our interconnected, globalised world, described in Box 7.1.

Box 7.1: A word about globalisation

Globalisation has several definitions, but broadly it refers to the interconnectedness of the world. Advances in physical modes of transport over the last few centuries started this connectivity. The digital communications revolution of the last 30 years has accelerated this spectacularly. Consequently, there is unprecedented movement of knowledge, ideas and trade between nations and cultures. This includes mass media and popular culture which can reach global communities in real time.

In practice, throughout modern history globalisation has involved richer countries expanding trade to serve global markets. Firms within these richer countries have also been keen to engage knowledge and labour more cheaply and this has often been available in other, less rich, countries. As a result, the ideas and methodologies of business and work have, to a large extent, been transferred from mostly Western countries in North America and Europe (and including parts of Oceania) to many other regions. Indeed, the most dominant of these, North America, has transferred business models and practices to other Western countries too. Alongside this is the transfer of culture. With global markets, media, news and information transferring around the world in real time, and Western popular culture, including language, music and literature, permeating and pervading on a global scale, the most dominant Western culture has spread throughout the world in a way not matched by other cultures, and indeed often causes cultural contraction at a local level.

Globalisation thus includes both positive and negative effects, and these are felt unequally depending on where you are in the world. The advantages of globalisation include:

- trade and communications being improved;
- people being more connected;
- efficiency gains for businesses and employment opportunities for people.

On the other hand, disadvantages may also be summarised:

- local cultures can experience a diminishing effect as a (foreign) dominant culture spreads;

- there is inequity in the distribution of wealth and opportunity;
- there is potential for (and experience of) exploitation of the people of some countries and cultures by those of another.

These negative effects can (and do) lead to backlash, expressed variably depending on local culture and, in some cases, the extent of disadvantage. For some countries and cultures there may be specific interventions to maintain local and traditional cultures, such as promotion of local language use and investment in local cultural offerings. In other countries and cultures there may be more robust, even violent, rejection of non-local culture and values. These responses are not limited to rest-of-the-world versus Western culture, though. First, non-dominant local Western cultures have experienced similar diminishment to that of non-Western cultures. Second, Western domination is characteristic of our recent global history. Globalisation may have started with a dominant Western affect, but the future may not see continued valorisation of Western ideas.

PERSPECTIVES FROM PRACTICE 7.3

Jannie Tam reflected on her time of working in MNEs and the need for bridging cultural expectations and practices:

> When I worked for Disney and the others, we really had to fight for attention because they're a global brand, they have so many different markets to look after. A simple document like a legal document, you have to queue for your turn. But everything is urgent for us, right? So we have to be vocal and also stress the importance to avoid the consequences of not getting it done. We have our own Asian ways of doing business. Basically it's a lot of trust and if we don't deliver the trust breaks and then it's going to be hard in the long run. So we have to be able to tell them this is a sensitive area and what are the deal breakers basically, according to our culture and practice. I was sitting in the regional office in Hong Kong so I had to represent the Asian culture back to the States, the headquarters, but also regionally. I also had to be sensitive about all the different subcultures like Southeast Asia, very different from mainlanders. We also have to be sensitive about the local culture and understand their priorities. And then I had to basically digest and convert that into something that was easy to comprehend from the head office in the Western setting.

(Continued)

Victor Ikande discussed a similar translation role between cultures in his leadership position in the Middle East:

> If there's any place that my cultural background as Nigerian and British has benefited me, it's right now in the Middle East. I see some unique alignments in behaviours with what I've grown up with in Nigeria and I believe that is an advantage. So shouting is not a big deal for me because that's what we all do in Nigeria, you know, it's a lot louder, and mannerisms are more animated, and things like that. So I found that I maybe have had less of a cultural shock compared to someone who has never been out of the Western culture. I found that there was a lot of that external behaviour and it was very similar to what I was used to. So I think that helped me quite a bit in my current roles in the Middle East. And I see things a bit differently insofar as when you look at the situation, you are able to understand something because you just situationalise it in terms of how it works in Nigeria and you can get to that level of perception that maybe would have not been possible if I didn't have that cultural background. So, I'll give you a good example. Somebody tells me, 'My uncle is sick, I need to be off work for two weeks'. That might sound bizarre to you, but I get it. I get how that can happen where an uncle is sick so you can't come to work because we've got to make sure everything goes well. But corporate-wise it is only first relatives, immediate family, that counts. But I can understand why somebody needs to take time off because an uncle is sick or has passed away, because they have to settle the family business and all that. I get that and I'm not shocked when somebody comes to me and we have to deal with that. But it's not very Western if you know what I mean. For Indians and Middle Easterns the family goes a bit wider. It can be tricky because Hollins want a consistent culture. They want a consistent message, regardless. So you have to deal with it on a very individual level, trying to be flexible where you feel that there is a genuine reason. So it's more than anything about decision-making because at a corporate level there is absolutely no room to breathe. So you deal with it with your own authority based on a personal decision of leeway and understanding with the person on how to work around it, so perhaps remote working or time in lieu.

Claire McCarthy describes similar methods of managing corporate policy in a way that allows her to lead with some cultural sensitivity:

> Cardiff is a diverse city so we have a lot of mix in our staff group, not just religious and ethnic but also different socio-economic backgrounds. We also have different sexualities and things. But our donor group and our support group and the beneficiary group are also really diverse. Generally we would put it to one side in terms of the way we approach policy and leadership protocol. But we are sensitive. I'm conscious of the fact that we have people of

different religions, for example, and I don't want to single them out and make a big hoopla about it because I think that can be just really unwelcome. But at the same time, I accept that some of them will want time off at certain points in the year and they will be different from the traditional holidays we might want and I will accommodate that absolutely.

Perspectives from practice questions

1. Why was it important for Jannie to translate and 'convert' regional cultural practices to headquarters when she worked for large Western media companies?
2. How does Victor's Nigerian cultural background inform his leadership in the Middle East?
3. Why do you think that Claire and Victor are keen to accommodate cultural differences?
4. Do you think that Victor diverging from the corporate policy of allowing time off work only for crises in immediate family is appropriate?
5. If your clients (or beneficiaries in Claire's case) are diverse from a cultural point of view, is it important to have leaders from those cultures?

More now than ever before, a leader in a globalised and interconnected world needs to know how different people view and experience life and work and have some intelligent engagement with that. More broadly, to understand the environment in which they are leading, those in leadership roles should account for cultural nuances in:

*   the industrial or sectoral environment;
*   the political and economic context;
*   the culture of the society, with its specific norms and values, as they affect the people in the organisation;
*   variations within that culture, such as gender, age, education level, wealth, even race and ethnicity.

In terms of *leading people*, there may be variation in how we express emotions, how we relate to each other, how we communicate criticism and praise. As discussed in Chapter 8 on ethics, there may also be variation in our expectations of work and our levels of commitment to work and non-work activities. There may be specific etiquette associated with business and other types of organisations that might involve, for example, networks and reciprocity. If respect and trust are key to leading people, a leader cannot rely on cultural stereotypes. Instead, the ability to learn and develop strategies for meaningful engagement are critical elements in cross-cultural leadership.

Similarly, when it comes to *thought leadership*, an organisation's leaders have to balance the values and norms of the organisation with those of the intercultural context. This may not always be possible. Sometimes this will even involve structural barriers, such as regulations (for example, you may perceive a great opportunity to open a bar or start a distillery, but it won't gain much traction in a country that prohibits the manufacture and sale of alcohol). There also may be many organisational values that are incongruent with cultural norms and values, and indeed alternatively there can be cultural divergence that contravenes core values of an organisation. If alignment cannot be achieved, then leadership might involve a decision for an organisation *not* to operate in that cultural context. Where alignment is possible, adaptation of the offering, of the strategy and of the operations of the organisation may be necessary. For example, consider the restrictions on trading imposed inconsistently on different religious holidays throughout the world, or the need for global franchises to comply with cultural rules on food manufacture. These examples illustrate the need for convergent approaches to leading organisations in remote (from head-office) cultural contexts.

LEADERSHIP AND CULTURE AT ITS SIMPLEST

Culture is the common beliefs and behaviours of a group of people.

Cultures vary geographically, temporally and generationally, and in other ways too.

To enable the trust, transformational and relational qualities of leadership, an understanding of the cultural context is necessary.

Cultural dimensions theories and other approaches to understanding cultural variation help inform leadership, though leaders must caution against generalising and stereotyping.

Globalisation and increased digital connectivity have increased the need for cross-cultural awareness amongst leaders.

Intercultural leaders have access to opportunities born of cross-cultural knowledge, and challenges in terms of strategising and leading people.

Cross-cultural leadership involves analysing and balancing fit between cultures, including that of the organisation.

SUMMARY

This chapter has explored some of the key issues regarding the different expressions and experiences of culture. This is often understood as regionally varying, but it may also relate temporally to generations or to some other distinguisher between people. Cultural diversity throughout the world is what gives humanity its richness. Globalisation and the success of market-based economic systems have threatened some of the diversity. Certainly, some compliance is required if we are to operate within consistent structures around the world, such as having recognised education systems, robust rules on payments and finance, and reliable institutions to support trade and other types of social connectedness. But there is room for diversity too, and organisations and leaders that are mindful of that will find that opportunities and engagement of effort are enabled by reasoned consideration of best fit and best approaches to inter-cultural issues. There are implications in terms of values and ethics, and an organisation's engagement with a culture and the treatment of people by leaders in organisations require careful ethical reasoning. The next chapter explores this further.

EXERCISES

Give an explanation of culture and some examples of cultural variation.

Consider your own organisation or one you have experienced in the past. Does it have cultural variation? How is this handled by the leadership of the organisation?

To what extent do you think your views of another culture may be stereotypical?

What are the dangers of relying on stereotypes of cultures?

Give an explanation of cultural dimensions theories.

How useful do you think cultural dimensions theories are for MNEs and otherwise culturally diverse organisations?

What are the limitations of cultural dimensions theories?

What are the implications for practitioners in terms of leading in multicultural environments?

Do you think there is a relationship between culturally sensitive leadership and motivations amongst followers?

8
LEADING AND ETHICS

INTRODUCTION

In this chapter we explore some of the issues associated with leadership and ethics. Ethics is perhaps the single most important part of being a leader, whether that be expressed as *thought leadership* or *leading people*. Ethical leadership requires reasoning and judgement based on principles and beliefs, and in organisations includes the balancing of economic interests with social responsibilities. This chapter is written at a time where there are two major agendas at play in the world. The first of these is the treatment of people. The second is the climate emergency. As outlined in Chapter 1, these two broad agendas underpin much of the philosophy and detail of the UN's commitment to sustainable development. Launched in 2015, *Agenda 2030* is the UN's call to action for governments and private, public and third-sector organisations, and for individuals, to commit to developing '*a world of universal respect for human rights and human dignity, the rule of law, justice, equality and non-discrimination*'. The 17 goals are shown in Figure 8.1. These have prompted commitment to change throughout nations and amongst organisations in all commercial sectors.

Ethics has always been important of course, but a global focus on sustainable development has prompted ethical reflection and practice in a way not seen in previous generations. The role, behaviours and values of leaders are front and centre in the analysis of ethical practice and conduct in organisations. The following sections explore some of the key issues.

MORALITY, LEADING AND DEFINING 'GOOD LEADERSHIP'

The English language uses the word 'good' to mean a variety of things. There are countless cases, historical and contemporary, of superb leadership, but where the ideas, intentions

Figure 8.1   The UN Sustainable Development Goals[1]

Source: www.un.org/sustainabledevelopment/.

and outcomes of that leadership are judged to have been deleterious, the *effects* of the leader have had negative, sometimes devastating, consequences for economies and societies. Thus, never is the distinction between meanings of the word 'good' more pertinent than when applied to leadership. They are explained below:

- *good leadership*: effective, efficient, well deployed;
- *leadership for good*: virtuous leadership, leadership to contribute to the greater good, values-based and moral leadership.

This chapter focuses on the second definition: leadership that is ethically informed and cognizant of the well-being and welfare of stakeholders.

There is no straightforward distinction between being a good person while leading or a bad person while leading. In fact, notions of morality, of right and wrong, good and bad, vary enormously from one person to another. There are absolutes of course; most of humanity agrees on such things as the right to life, the right to freedom, the right to personal ownership. Sources of moral guidance, such as humanist or religious doctrine or personal rationality, align and overlap with these absolutes in so far as they define violation of these rights as 'wrong'. Beyond the absolutes, though, there are infinite shades of grey when it comes to notions of good versus bad, right versus wrong. These are influenced

[1]The content of this publication has not been approved by the United Nations and does not reflect the views of the United Nations or its officials or Member States.

by social and cultural backgrounds and situations, family and network influences, and of course the formal structural and legislative environment. As such, ethics are often nuanced and variable from one person to another and from one society to another. This variation is rationalised throughout the world's various intellectual traditions. Here we refer to the Western principles of *ethical relativism*.

Box 8.1: A word about ethical relativism

The Western concept of relativism has its roots in classical philosophy. The ancient Greek philosopher Socrates is recognised as the father of Western philosophy, including moral philosophy and ethics. He explored the idea of virtue by challenging people to reflect on and examine how they arrive at their understanding of it. Consequently, Socrates is considered the instigator of the idea of *cultural relativism*, which allows that interpretations of reality may vary based on people's different beliefs and values, which are influenced by their social culture. These different interpretations of reality lead people in different cultural settings to have different perspectives (outside of absolutes) on what is right and wrong, good and bad, and these perspectives in turn inform behaviours.

According to a relativist position, right and wrong are not 'fixed' at a conceptual level and so ethics as understood and demonstrated by different people may vary. Just as culture varies (as noted in Chapter 7), so too can ethics vary geographically and temporally. These are explored in turn below.

Geographic variation

As proposed by Socrates, in different regions values and morals are not consistent. While there are often more consistencies than divergences, the behaviours of people in different regions of the world can demonstrate their different perspectives on what is considered ethical. This can affect ethics in society and these can be replicated into organisations.

Let's take an example: a common source of divergent practice in organisational life – attributed to ethical positions – is the use of personal and social networks for career advancement. The use of these is variously considered ethical and unethical depending on the cultural norms of the society you live in. For example, the term *nepotism* is defined as the act of conferring unfair advantage to relatives. *Cronyism* is a similar term that refers to the favouring of personal and social contacts. Broadly speaking, in the Northern and Western parts of the world, both nepotism and cronyism are used to imply unethical and even reprehensible practices (to the point that legislation against such practices applies in some places). Elsewhere, though, there are all sorts of customs that refer to the use of personal and social networks, and these can include matters that relate to work and to organisations. *Wasta* in the Middle East and North Africa (MENA), *guanxi* in China, *ubuntu* in sub-Saharan Africa – while each is different (and, indeed, each can be expressed differently even within the broad regions with which they are identified), they all point to participation and contribution in networks or groups, including amongst relatives and contacts (e.g. Barnett et al., 2013 on *wasta*, Broodryk, 2005 on *ubuntu* and Guo et al., 2018 on *guanxi*). In particular, each of these examples (and there are others throughout the world) refers to social and cultural practices that involve the development and deployment of social capital, and include the application of favour and reciprocity. In particular in business studies, social practices such as these have been found to advantage people in work and organisations (e.g. Newenham-Kahindi, 2009 on the effect of *ubuntu* on business in Tanzania; Banu et al., 2020 on *wasta* in the Middle East). Rather than being frowned upon, these practices can be understood to be ethically benign or even virtuous since the underpinning rationale is that we have a collective responsibility to each other, at least to some degree.

Box 8.2: Definitions

The Urban Dictionary (2021) defines:

Nepotism as 'the act of using power or influence to get good jobs or unfair advantages for members of your own family'.

Cronyism as 'particularity to friends expressed by appointment of them to positions of authority, regardless of their qualifications'.

Wasta as an Arabic word that means favouritism that applies 'the influence of relatives or acquaintances to achieve objectives'.

Guanxi as a Chinese concept associated with 'personalized networks of influence ... based on the exchange of favours in a system of social networks and influential relationships'.

Ubuntu as 'an African phrase meaning humanity towards others'.

The variation in experiences of group membership and the use of social contacts is entirely cultural. In fact, there is resonance with the distinction made in *cultural dimensions theories*, described in Chapter 7, between individualistic cultures and collectivist ones. Cultures that prioritise the interests of the individual tend to frown upon preferential treatments (at least formally and officially), while cultures that prioritise responsibilities to the society or community are more likely to regard preferential treatment as either ethically neutral or even as a duty. In fact, of course, none of these approaches is objectively 'right' or 'wrong'; rather they are perceived as one or the other depending on the cultural context in question.

Temporal variation

Attitudes, morals and values can change over time. The values in any region of the world that were held in the historical past are often quite alien to the values of people today. Even within living memory, ethical variation can be observable. In some cases, this is because there is access to information that was not available in the past. For example, smoking cigarettes had no ethical loading in European nations in the past, but now, because we know of the damage it does to health and to the health of others, there can be ethical judgement imposed on cigarette manufacturers, cigarette marketing and even individual smokers that was inconceivable in previous generations. Similar judgements are now made in industries such as energy and fast food for similar reasons – that we now understand better the impacts of these industries and this new understanding has brought with it a change in how (some) people perceive the ethics of the production and consumption of these products. There are countless examples in the connected world of today, where greater amounts of information about social, political and organisational life have informed changes in the ethical stance of populations. The digitally enhanced interconnected world enables observation of and empathy with the effects on people's lives of attitudes, practices, traditions and, of course, business and other organisations, and these cause changes in attitudes and ethical perspectives.

Sometimes, though, there is no obvious reason for temporal variation in values and ethics. A good example of this is the change in North American and some European attitudes towards the manufacture, sale and wearing of fur. There are many people who will remember (perhaps still own) fur coats, hats, gloves. They will remember how it was associated with glamour and wealth and fashion, and a common aspiration was to own fur apparel. The grandchildren of these same people may well be utterly opposed to the use of fur as a fashion statement. The ethical change in perspective on this topic has led to a decline in that industry as greater amounts of people boycott it. The argument is often associated with animal cruelty or the misuse of animals for superficial or vanity-related consumption. But the point here is that knowledge about this has not changed over the years – it has always been known by suppliers and consumers that the fur comes from animals and that the luxury market is served. Indeed, there are also other types of apparel – shoes for example – that continue to be mass produced in leather, but this is not subject to the same ethical loading.

Elsewhere, there are countless examples of older generations that disapprove on some moral grounds with the behaviours of younger ones. Often these are related to the extent to which traditions are flouted, or the norms of the past updated consequent to new technologies or, again, more information. Sometimes it is possible to see why there is a moral imposition on some behaviours – perhaps stemming from religious or other rules or traditions – and sometimes it seems quite random (consider how each generation has disapproved sequentially of too much reading, not enough reading, rock music, television, computer games and social media).

Thus, while there may be scores of different perspectives on ethics as they vary temporally, it is often not possible to say in an absolute way that one generation is right and one is wrong. Most often they are embedded in contexts such that one's morals or ethical position cannot be understood separately from one's context within a society and culture. There are exceptions of course: there can be little defence of the ethical positions of slavers for example, nor indeed the complicity and silence of others. But broadly speaking, ethics are a part of the human state that involves conscience, values and the analysis of information and knowledge, and these vary by society, culture and individual.

At its simplest: Ethical relativisim refers to variation in moral perspectives based on cultural context.

LEADING AND ETHICAL VARIATION

The implications for leaders of variation in ethical perspectives and behaviours include that there is a need for analysis of a situation. Leaders have conscience and ethical perspectives too, though, and so decisions and practices have to achieve a balance between what is personally acceptable, what is compliant and aligned with organisational values, and the ethics and practices of the socio-culture of followers and other stakeholders. This is complex and requires reasoning and reflection of some sophistication. Thus, in leadership situations, reasoning and judgement based on principles and beliefs are required, but in organisations there also has to be a balance with economic interests and social responsibilities.

Leading ethically, therefore, involves consideration of:

* the social and cultural context;
* company ethics or organisational values;
* personal ethics.

The various issues associated with developing ethical organisational practices are a significant role and responsibility of leadership. It is to the challenges and practices of ethical leadership *within* organisations that we turn to next.

ETHICAL LEADERSHIP PRACTICE *WITHIN* ORGANISATIONS

Leaders, by definition, are almost always in a privileged position in terms of having elevated status amongst co-workers. That brings with it specific responsibilities. Just as equality, sustainability and ethical behaviours in general are encouraged at a macro level for organisations, so too do they have specific application *within* organisations.

Leadership in organisations is essentially relational in one form or another. Whether communicating *thought leadership* through strategy and ideas or involving *leading people*, communications and relations are critical. That being the case, the ethical behaviour of leaders is important.

First, as *thought leaders*, there is a responsibility to be seen to be doing the right thing. As theorised, particularly in *transformational leadership theory* in its *inspirational motivation/charisma* pillar, but elsewhere too, there is emphasis on the conduct of leaders being such that others might emulate them. If one is to be a role model, there is a responsibility to be a good (virtuous) one. Historical and modern examples of great leadership for destructive purposes show how a leader's ideology and behaviours can enable and act to justify destructive behaviours in others – apart from wars and exploitation, think of recent financial scandals and industry cover-ups where the quality of the moral decisions amongst leaders infected whole organisations and sectors (Padilla et al., 2007 explores some of these). This follows through into *leading people*: if followers perceive that the conduct of a leader is ethically dubious, then they may regard this as a precedent and model of behaviours. From there, a cascade effect can follow, leading to an organisational culture described as toxic.

There have been many studies of toxic leadership, including those that relate to the dissemination of toxic ideas and those that relate to the more common organisational problem of creating a toxic workplace. In a recent article, Laguda (2021) reviews the literature throughout organisation studies on toxic leadership, finding unethical behaviours

Table 8.1 Examples of toxic leadership in practice

The shouter	Barks orders, lacks manners, rarely says please or thank you, scares people, is unapproachable and blame-oriented
The humiliator	Close relation of the shouter, but does not necessarily raise voice. Undermines, criticises and embarrasses, face to face and behind back
The micromanager	Scrutinises work, directs operations even at detail levels, discourages autonomy, monitors performance for errors
The *ad infinitum* delegator	Allows autonomy and can praise, but piles work and responsibility on to the point that followers are stressed and overwhelmed
The interrogator	May afford autonomy, but scrutinises with a view to finding fault. Requires copious explanations and justification for followers' decisions

at the heart. Laguda uses extant research to explore different ways in which leaders can affect performance, and reports consistent evidence of negative organisational effects. Behaviours that marginalise, diminish or restrict followers in particular are charged with prompting reduction or withdrawal of participation amongst employees and other followers. In essence of course, this is not leadership – it is definitionally the opposite of leadership if that is understood to involve enabling best effort from people, and so, as per discussions in Chapters 1 and 4, what is actually described is *toxic headship*. Regardless, though, organisations can have heads/leaders who act in toxic ways. Five common types are summarised in Table 8.1.

PERSPECTIVES FROM PRACTICE 8.1

Claire McCarthy is the Director of Operations and HR at a large children's charity in Wales. More information about Claire can be found on page 2.

Ken Lorenz is the owner of a data analytics firm and a data analytics consultancy, both based in the USA. More information about Ken can be found on page 2.

Victor Ikande is a regional head for the US-based construction firm Hollins. More information about Victor can be found on page 3.

Claire McCarthy in the UK charity sector makes reference to the damage favouritism, as a type of toxic leadership, can do in an organisation:

> In terms of sucking up, there's always a bit of that that's reasonably enjoyable because you think, 'Good, the fact that you're a suck-up means I can probably ask you to do things and you'll do them'. But the difficulty is that what they won't do is challenge your ideas. So they're good on one hand because you can give them work to do and they're going to do their best for you, but on the flip side they're not necessarily going to tell you about problems because they don't want to criticise you. Also, if others in the team are seeing that ... I mean you have to make sure that you don't treat them differently, that you treat everybody in the same way, and you don't give all the best jobs to the suck-up. I think it's about how you handle yourself at work, and I always keep a decent arm's length.

In the private sector, Ken Lorenz similarly applies leadership in a way that is informed by experience of leading in an ethical way. As identified in Chapter 3, he considers an environment where people are not able to speak candidly for fear of reprisal as a potentially significant limitation to business, and this is particularly important for his data analytics

(Continued)

enterprises. Consequently, his leadership is informed so as to mitigate this limitation. Speaking with reference specifically to a USA cultural context he notes:

> I don't think anyone wants to give you bad news or say that this isn't working right. So you have to go look for it. If you just question, 'How's everything going, is everything working?', then they'll tell you about problems they see. But you have to push to get those things. No one wants to say this isn't working. They'll complain to their peers but they won't tell management there's a problem. In previous jobs I had there was definitely a culture of good news only and it was very damaging.

Ken also noted how destructive poor behaviours of leaders can be on performance:

> We had one partner that just came in and yelled because that was the way he wanted to run his part of the business and that was the way he said he could motivate the call centre – to come in and tell them they were doing a bad job and they needed to do better. And I got lots of complaints from the employees and people were wanting to leave because nothing they did was right. It was so demoralising. We asked him not to come to the office and told him, 'You can't do this anymore because people want to leave'. I think if people are yelling at work, you've lost sight of the fact we are just at work. You don't need to yell at people.

More pragmatically, Victor Ikande also refers to ethical leadership as a means by which strategic and operational goals are met. He explains it thus:

> The people that I would consider not to have led properly, they did not have the focus on cultivating. They led by fear. The led by lack of engagement and, ultimately, they drove tasks, which gave them short term gains but overall there was an overall failure at the end. I've never been on a project that made money where motivation was poor, where people were afraid on the job. No matter how hard they worked, the projects that I've been on that lost money for the businesses were those that had those attributes: lack of trust, fear amongst the people, everybody trying to cover their back. And then no matter how hard [a leader] drove, they usually ended up making a loss. Projects that I find to be successful are where people are happy and there is a feel-good factor around the project.

Perspectives from practice questions

1. Why does Claire consider it important to allow people to speak and to criticise without fear of repercussions?
2. What are the limitations for Ken's business of not having the ability to speak openly about problems?

3. In what ways do you think the 'culture of no bad news' that Ken describes might damage a firm?
4. How would you deal with a leader who shouts and intimidates as Ken describes?
5. Do you think Victor's observation that environments that are toxic produce lower performance than environments that are supportive is true in your experience or industry or organisation?

The toxic types described in the testimonies and in Table 8.1 above are entirely counter-productive in terms of leadership. Throughout this book, there has been note of the effectiveness of *transformational* and *relational* approaches to leadership. Trust is central to the successful deployment of these approaches. Indeed, even where other styles are applied – such as *directive* or newer forms of *shared* and *distributed leadership* – the ability to achieve compliance and engagement from followers still relies on the extent to which a leader is trusted. That being the case, a leader has to create an environment for followers that is conducive to effective relationships and trust and this involves behaviours that are ethical. People who find their jobs demotivating and stressful will do one of two things: reduce engagement or withdraw it by leaving. This represents a cost to an organisation, and this comprises one part of the most pragmatic rationales for ethical leadership: the business case, which along with the moral case, is outlined in the next section on rationalising ethical leadership.

RATIONALISING ETHICAL LEADERSHIP

There are two main ways to rationalise why ethical leadership is so important in organisations. Like all other spheres of life, there is moral imperative. In addition to that, there are more pragmatic rationales for why organisations in particular must be led with ethics as a core concern. If we return to the UN's Sustainable Development Goals again as an example set of ethical challenges, it is clear that there is a moral underpinning. But they also respond to pragmatic issues facing the world today. For example, response to climate problems can be defined not only as moral, but also as a means by which to manage finite resources with a view to sustaining life. Similarly, while there is a moral imperative to encourage equality, there is also a pragmatic case that equality in societies and organisations creates opportunities borne of diverse participation (as discussed in Chapter 6). Thus, ethics is not always just about philanthropy and altruism. There are also rationales for the application of ethical practices that resonate with utilitarian principles (being of use and benefit for individuals and groups) and even egoism (being motivated by self-interest). The terms used here refer to Western philosophy and moral development, but are echoed in other intellectual and cultural traditions too. The aim here is not to critique these, but instead to use the broad ideas to inform what this means for leaders. In this section, therefore, we explore the reasons why ethical considerations in organisations are so important. Here, as for the cultural sensitivity discussed in Chapter 7, we explore this through both *the moral case* and *the business case*.

The moral case

There is a moral underpinning of all organisational ambitions to act in an ethical manner. The purpose of most organisations is to achieve some business, public or charitable aims. For that pursuit to be ethical, it cannot be at the expense of that which is considered morally acceptable. Thus, without making any other case, virtue is an end in itself and comprises a key pillar in organisational strategies and operations.

The business case

The unethical behaviours summarised in Table 8.1 in this chapter are anathema to the ideals of leadership theorised and observed in modern organisations. Autonomy and trust and relationships are entirely undermined by these types of behaviours, rendering disadvantage for organisations since people are not supported to develop and excel, and best effort is not enabled.

Consumer protection	**The working environment**
• Product safety • Non-exploitation	• Health and safety • Discrimination and harassment
Examples: poisoning customers; increasing debt or poverty for vulnerable people ***Risk***: consumer injury, illegality, prosecution, lack of repeat custom, bad publicity, loss of market share	***Example***: worker protective equipment and clothing in chemical industries ***Risk***: worker detriment, illegality, prosecution, bad publicity, loss of market share
Environmental responsibility	**Choice of partners**
• Safe and appropriate use of natural resources • Safe use and disposal of non-natural resources • What are the local and global impacts?	• Suppliers, distributors, other partnerships • Are they compliant with the values of the organisation?
Example: irresponsible disposal of chemicals ***Risk***: personnel and neighbour injury, environmental injury, illegality, prosecution, bad publicity, loss of market share	***Example***: ethical labour practices ***Risk***: bad publicity, loss of market share

Figure 8.2 Ethics, stakeholder and business risk examples

Other business or mission critical issues are affected by the ethical conduct of leaders too. All organisations have multiple stakeholders, including staff (followers), partners, shareholders, clients or customers, neighbours, competitors, suppliers, wider locale and wider society. Leaders must balance the effects of the organisation and their decisions on all of these simultaneously. Failure to act ethically in any area can have negative, even disastrous results. Figure 8.2 illustrates some example scenarios.

Figure 8.2 summarises only a few scenarios that leaders in organisations have to consider. It is included merely to illustrate the complexity of ethical decision-making in organisational contexts, and particularly as they affect the business or mission of the organisation.

Increasingly also, businesses have responsibilities that transcend their immediate stakeholders. These include their need to engage with global challenges and the UN's sustainability goals. Consequently, organisations are currently broadly represented by three types:

- businesses and other organisations that are created in order to *engage direct* with a global challenge or local sustainability issue;
- businesses or other organisations that *apply* sustainability principles (environmental or humanitarian) in, for example, decisions regarding supply chains, operational practices, corporate social responsibility (CSR) or other social contributions, either from inception or as part of a change programme;
- businesses that *do not engage* with sustainability.

Currently all three of these types of organisation are common. Increasingly, though, organisations that align with Type 1 or Type 2 or a combination of both are gaining market share because of concurrent changes in ethics and values in modern society. As such, ethical leadership in organisations is not just about avoiding poor ethical decisions that will have negative business outcomes, but is also about applying ethics commensurate with cultural values that can act to create opportunities to *gain* new markets and increase market share. This is not new; there are examples of the use of morality to serve markets throughout history. This includes businesses that engage ethics-driven tastes, such as vegetarianism, anti-vivisectionism, ethical finance – and, of course, the evocation of ethics and virtue is a central underpinning of most donation-based charities. Increasingly, though, sustainability and ethical practices are underpinning opportunities in diverse industries that have little or no ethical precedence. The most likely reasons for this is that the information and knowledge brought about by global connectivity and specific initiatives, such as the UN's SDGs, have heightened awareness of ethical issues and changed the way people interact with organisations. This has heightened the demand in markets and throughout wider society for ethics to be demonstrably and consistently informing organisational practice.

The modern widespread awareness and sensitivity to ethics requires ethical leadership that is informed by reason and judgement and involving all stakeholders. But the organisation is a stakeholder too. Central to ethical judgements, therefore, is doing the right thing by the organisation. In public and third-sector organisations this means staying within budgets; if this is not achieved then the organisation will fail. For businesses, this means achieving profit, as discussed in Box 8.3.

Box 8.3: A word about profit

In market systems, the purpose of commercial enterprises is to trade at profit, where profit is defined as the financial difference between the cost of owning, transforming and supplying an offering and the price charged to the customer to consume it. This is the underpinning of capitalism. Profits create funds for future opportunities and profit is a foundational principle of business. Without profit, a business cannot prevail. It cannot continue to create the offering if there are no funds with which to do this.

Profit is, in and of itself, neither ethical nor unethical. What has perhaps slanted views on profit-seeking is greed, where the pursuit of profit trumps all other considerations. Many businesses over the years and in the present day are charged with unethical profiteering. In corporates, responsibilities to shareholders are argued to be a top priority, and again this has its critics in so far as the alternative view is that customers or other stakeholders and/or other agendas should be prioritised. Striking a balance of these competing interests is one of the challenges of ethical leadership, and in particular balancing the pursuit of profit with other responsibilities. But profit itself is not unethical. As the underpinning of private business and the market economy, it is the key economic antecedent that creates jobs, contributes gross domestic product and pays tax, which is then spent on welfare, health, education, infrastructure such as roads and utility supply, and so on. Indeed, in market economies, a lack of profit is unethical since profit is what funds ongoing employment, providing people with incomes with which to furnish lives (the same is true of the ethical need to maintain compliant budgets in the public and third sectors). Without incomes there is poverty, and poverty is unethical.

The ethical dilemmas with profit are therefore how it is used and the extent to which it is prioritised above other considerations. This is why in many countries there are strict rules about how profit is managed and applied, often legislated within parameters that are considered ethically acceptable within that national culture.

There can be a perception of conflict between the pursuit of organisational goals – especially profit – and acting ethically. Part of the complexity of leadership is the management of this conflict. As outlined in Box 8.3, the challenge for leaders therefore is achieving ethical *balance*.

Balancing the interests of the organisational, stakeholders' and wider social values includes cognizance of the conduct of others in the organisation too. This may involve elements of leadership that can be the most challenging – where the conduct of individuals may not be congruent with the aims and values of the organisation. For leaders, this can often compel difficult conversations and difficult decisions. Some of our participant leaders provide some candid testimony below.

PERSPECTIVES FROM PRACTICE 8.2

With reference to his businesses in travel and in data analytics, Ken Lorenz has utilised call centres as a part of the business models. It is in this context that he related the following:

> There's a lot of opportunity for fraud in the call centre world. I had to watch for that all the time and go through the numbers and track things. For example, for the travel company they [the staff] could get bonused on sales targets but we had people who were getting people to buy tickets and then returning them. So they would still get the bonus but the sale was fraudulent. These people were faking the bonus. So I had to confront them and I had to fire a bunch of people for it.

Poor ethical behaviour is not the exclusive preserve of the people who work in the private sector of course. Indeed, in a previous third-sector organisation, Claire McCarthy recounted a case of recurrent theft from the charity's accounts by a member of staff. This person was confronted, dismissed, tried and eventually convicted through the judicial system.

Perspectives from practice questions

1. If you were Ken or Claire, how would you have dealt with the situations they encountered?
2. Where do you think the lines are in terms of ethical conduct in your organisation?

REVIEWING ETHICS

The modern interconnected and ethically aware market throughout the world means that consumers and organisational leaders are more conscious than ever before about ethical issues. This has prompted many organisations to commit to ethical practices in response to demand from markets and in response to socio-culturally informed organisational and personal ethics. There are myriad ways organisations can and do engage in ethical practices, and various lenses through which they can interrogate their systems, processes and procedures from an ethical perspective. Here we refer to the ESG framework because it neatly captures three of the broad ethical challenges most organisations face.

Referring to ethical conduct in the three broad categories of *environment, society* and *governance*, the ESG framework has its origins in the 1970s' and 1980s' corporate America. In particular, it was developed within the global finance sector as a means by which to facilitate ethical investing. Since then, many different industries throughout the world have adopted the key principles of ESG as a way of analysing their operations and of monitoring and even measuring these from an ethical perspective. Countless studies have explored the links between adherence to ESG principles and performance. Many of these are specific to investment (such as a recent article by Pedersen et al., 2021). More broadly, Friede et al. (2015) present a good meta-study across the range of the corporate world.

The component elements of ESG are summarised in Box 8.4.

Box 8.4: The ESG lens

Environmental: This category includes contribution to addressing the climate emergency, but other environmental issues too. For example, an organisation may be prompted to explore its engagement with sustainability, circular principles (the practices of reusing, recycling, repurposing for materials, inputs and waste and other outputs), and environment-related practices amongst partners and throughout supply chains and distribution channels.

Social: This category includes scrutiny of an organisation in terms of its effects on people and society. It prompts focus on human rights, equality and protection of consumers, but includes also other issues that affect the people in society. These include all the different ways in which ethics impact on humanity, either by directly affecting humans, or by affecting their sensibilities and sensitivities about things, such as the treatment of animals. As noted throughout this chapter, social-based ethical considerations may vary culturally and involve evolving morality amongst stakeholders, including leaders, employees, partners, clients and customers.

Governance: This refers to the way an organisation is run and how ethical the organisation is with regard to various issues associated with governance. This prompts inspection of things such as pay and conditions for employees, remuneration for shareholders, the backgrounds and other interests of shareholders or board members or trustees, the transparency of contracts with partners, suppliers and distributors, and any number of policies on matters that relate to potential for corruption, ranging from, for example, HR to intellectual property.

The relatively new approaches to analysing the ethical position of organisations in a systematic way have been embraced by the corporate world too. The term CSR – or corporate social responsibility – is also commonly associated with large organisations' attempts to comply with ethical requirements and ethical expectations of stakeholders. These may be formal – even departmentalised – processes in large businesses and public organisations, but even in small businesses and small third-sector organisations, greater emphasis on ethics is notable and the use of tools such as ESG to put some degree of systematisation into the inspection of ethics is increasing. Regardless of formality and size, the rationale behind these is that there is a will in organisations to practise – and importantly, be seen to practise – good ethics, consistent with the expectations of industry and markets. These refer to responsibilities outside the organisation, such as sustainability and equality as global issues, but also to practices within the organisation, affecting the leaders, staff, customers and neighbours.

Whether systematised or not, though, ethical leadership requires consideration and reflection. It requires that leaders apply an analysis of some sophistication that is cognizant of different stakeholders and perspectives and achieves balance of these sometimes competing interests.

PERSPECTIVES FROM PRACTICE 8.3

Jannie Tam is the founder of the Hong Kong-based talent development company GROWDynamics. More information about Jannie can be found on page 1.

John Black is a station manager with one of the UK's fire and rescue services. More information about John can be found on page 2.

Jannie Tam, John Black and Claire McCarthy all refer to ethics being important, and that leadership involves setting standards and being exemplary. Their testimonies below exemplify how they conduct their roles ethically:

> I think that one of the main things is to not go below a certain bar of behaviour yourself. And that can be really difficult because people get angry, people get stressed. If you can try to not go below a certain level of behaviours, I think that's a starting point. The other main thing is allowing people to tell you what's wrong without repercussions, to just cut to the chase, especially if they are unhappy about something, because misery can be infectious. (Claire)

> You have to be hands-on. It's very easy to be hands-off, but you have to be hands-on for people to trust you. Leaders who are hands-off are usually guided by the fact that they are lazy or not knowledgeable and so they delegate. Of course, often delegation is necessary and useful, but whether in the station or at fires or other incidents, some people delegate just to shirk their own responsibilities. And then the trust falls apart. (John)

(Continued)

I can't change any culture over time, but you can start from yourself, by being an ethical leader. And you have to genuinely care about people. You need to build this intrinsic trust. And at the same time you have to look at the shared vision and you bring the big picture to everyone. (Jannie)

Jannie also applies ESG as an analysis tool in her education and media business:

I'm not the president of the head office of a global brand but in your own office you can build a subculture. In terms of ESG, a multi-national enterprise needs to look at the market that they operate in. What are the cultural sensitivities? What are the social needs? But it's more than just being culturally sensitive. That is just the means. It's not the end, right. You also need to be a lot of other things in order to influence people, and that involves leading ethically, to make sure that people can give you trust. No matter what cultural background, if they find you ethical and trustworthy it's always easier. And that means you are transparent, and you look into the well-being of people who work with you or for you. These are very ESG things, right? For E, people need to come together to innovate in order that they can find sustainability [environmental] solutions in a commercially sensible way. So that is still depending on people. S is obvious: you need to lead and treat people well. S is how you treat people, how people feel like they are being looked after so they can flourish. Because oftentimes workplaces are the most toxic environments that one can be in. But I think nowadays, when ESG is so loud and clear, how can you not be treating people the way that they should be and not enabling people to flourish? The toxic environment needs to be controlled. But S is something that less corporates are focusing on simply because it's more abstract. How do you let people feel like you are really caring for the environment, caring for the people? That is very difficult to express and that is something even more difficult to execute.

Perspectives from practice questions

1. In what ways do Jannie and John and Claire express their responsibilities with regard to setting an ethical culture as leaders?
2. What do you think are the reasons Jannie refers to the ESG framework in her small business?
3. Do you think there are advantages to corporates and other larger organisations by adopting this as a lens for analysis?

LEADING AND ETHICS AT ITS SIMPLEST

Ethics relate to morality. While there are some absolutes and much consistency there can also be variation in what is considered ethical by different people.

Ethical variation can be cultural, geographic and/or temporal.

Leading ethically relates to *thought leadership* (via ideas and solutions) and *leading people* in organisations.

Both *thought leadership* and *leading people* can be toxic, though the toxic leading of people is oxymoronic and perhaps is more accurately described as toxic headship.

In organisations, the rationale for ethical leadership relates to both morals and pragmatic – often business-based – considerations.

Ethical leadership requires reflection and analysis involving personal values and consideration of others. In organisations, ethical leadership is inclusive of a range of stakeholders' interests and includes budgetary and profit imperatives.

SUMMARY

This chapter has explored the need for leaders to consider and reflect on the ethics of ideas and actions as they relate to leadership. It has shown that leadership is complex and only by applying reason and judgement can the decisions and actions of leaders be considered as ethically informed. The UN's Agenda 2030 gives some focus to the types of things leaders might be cognizant of, and frameworks such as ESG and CSR can be useful tools in terms of providing a systematic way of examining an organisation through an ethical lens. Beyond these there is the logic of serving increasingly ethically conscious markets and clients and creating welcoming and productive working environments. None of this is simple, and multiple interests must be considered. As such, a key challenge of leadership is the analysis of ethics and ethical balance in decision-making and practice, which are critical parts of the role and function of leadership in organisations.

EXERCISES

Explain the distinction between 'good leadership' and 'leadership for good'.

Give an explanation of ethics.

Give an explanation of ethical leadership.

What is ethical relativism?

Give some examples of ethical relativism in practice.

Can you think of any examples where:

- poor ethical judgements have been detrimental for an organisation;
- where the ethical position or actions have advantaged an organisation commercially?

Give an explanation of toxic leadership.

Reflect on your organisation. Do any of the behaviours in Table 8.1 resonate with your experience of a leader? What effect did this have on performance and morale?

Consider the example stakeholder-based ethical decision-making scenarios in Figure 8.2. Can you think of any examples in recent history where business was damaged by poor ethical conduct in any of these areas?

Why is ethics important for leaders?

9
DEVELOPING LEADERSHIP AND DEVELOPING LEADERS

INTRODUCTION

Throughout this book the key issues associated with knowledge and understanding about leading and leadership have been presented, alongside implications for practice and examples from real-life practitioners. Through these, the ways in which leadership might be developed are implied. In this chapter, this is collated and direct reference is made to how the content of the preceding chapters might be used to inform the development of leading for individuals and for the organisations in which they work.

There are countless manuals and courses available aimed explicitly at training the individual leader, sometimes context or industry specific, other times more general. Over the years, following much input from research, and especially psychology research, various tests and techniques to measure leadership and effectiveness have been developed so that organisations and the people in them can test their competencies and any skills gaps in terms of leadership, which of course may be mitigated with interventions and training. Useful as these are, they are not the focus of this chapter. Instead, this chapter collates information to focus on the ways that have been found in research and amongst practitioners to be effective means by which to develop leadership. As such there is focus on the individual leader, but there is also focus on the greater concept of developing leadership in organisations. This distinction is a relatively new one in terms of understanding leadership, in terms of developing skills and abilities for leading, and in terms of developing leadership in organisations. It marks a pertinent shift in focus from training individuals alone, and instead allows that leadership is something that occurs to everyone in some form in the organisation (whether experienced as a leader or as a follower). The following section describes how approaches to leadership development have evolved.

THE EVOLUTION OF LEADERSHIP DEVELOPMENT

Leadership is instrumental to organisations. The ways in which an organisation engages with its remit and sector are set by leadership, and leadership shapes the way people are treated and how they are influenced to make effort towards organisational goals. As noted throughout this book, leadership is one of the most critical elements that contribute to the distinctions between great performance, good performance and poor performance. Consequently, since the 1970s at least, when knowledge and understanding of leadership included that it is contextual and not merely a property of individuals, there has been much investment and effort in developing leadership within organisations and amongst personnel. Here it is presented in three distinct phases, informed by knowledge at the time.

The mid-twentieth century

As outlined in Chapter 2 of this book, prior to the mid-twentieth century leadership was studied, but it tended to be studied in terms of political or military campaigns and often took a *post hoc* or historical view with regard to what worked and what didn't. There was little crossover between these and the practices in public and commercial organisations. The middle decades of the twentieth century saw some advancement of knowledge and theorising about leadership, particularly in terms of character and behaviour, but it was only since the 1970s that research on leadership gained any real momentum. This was the point at which understanding had evolved to appreciate that leadership is a key factor in organisations, with the potential to affect the difference between good performance and bad performance; the difference between a thriving, surviving or failing organisation. Consequently, there was a significant increase in inspection and development of leadership theory and practice.

Early research in this period – around the 1960s–70s – was still very focused on the individual and their personality and behaviours (as discussed in Chapter 2). Consistent with this, therefore, was that leadership development in organisations had individual training front and centre, with a focus on developing the practices of leaders so that they might return to their organisations after training and be better prepared to direct followers. While context and follower sophistication (or readiness, as situational leadership theory would term it) were starting to be acknowledged as significant dimensions of leadership, there was little appreciation of the importance of any diversity amongst leaders (who, admittedly, at the time did tend to be pretty homogeneous in most countries, having been selected for 'headship' from a smaller pool than today). There was also little appreciation of the importance of diversity amongst followers. Instead, leaders (or more accurately in many cases, *heads*) were trained in order that they could enhance *their* careers as developed and experienced leaders in an organisation or sector.

The end of the twentieth century

By the end of the century, leadership development had been refined somewhat. Informed by key knowledge such as *contingency* and *situational* leadership theories (see Chapter 2) and *transformational leadership* measurements and ensuing theory, including the *Full Range of Leadership Model* (see Chapter 3), leadership development evolved. In particular, organisations were increasingly keen to develop leaders who would extract best effort from followers with a view to developing mutual excellence for people and for the organisation. While development still focused on the leader, there was much greater emphasis on understanding the importance of that leader's contribution. That included contribution through creativity and responsibility (what we refer to as *thought leadership* or envisioning throughout this book), and through influencing, supporting and developing followers (rather than coercing), as appropriate to task, job, context and follower ambitions (what we refer to as *leading people* throughout this book). Critical to this, according to scholars such as Bennis (1984), was that leaders had self-awareness and understood themselves, their strengths and their weaknesses. To these ends, consideration and understanding of oneself as a leader became popular means of development. These included increased interest in personality and other types of testing, such as Belbin's Self-Assessment Inventory (www.belbin.com) or the Myers–Briggs Type Indicator (www.myersbriggs.org) or the Dominance, Influence, Steadiness, Conscientiousness (DISC) personal assessment tool (www.discprofile.com) amongst others. These and other development courses and techniques also included at least some element of reflection on how one presents oneself as a leader and how that might be perceived by followers. The focus therefore was still on developing the leader, but with greater emphasis on the careers of people more generally (not just the leader's career) and on developing effective practices that would enhance performance of organisations (Turnbull James and Burgoyne, 2001).

The twenty-first century

The latest efforts to develop leadership refer to the most recent research and knowledge about it. Rather than focus on individuals exclusively (though there are still lots of development programmes and courses that do this), there is also emergence of development of leadership more generally in organisations. Informed by research, there is greater appreciation that everyone in the organisation is to some degree a stakeholder in how leadership is practised and how it is developed, and this is beginning to influence how organisations and trainers present and enable leadership development. In an early review of these new trends, Day (2001) describes how leadership development has moved from developing the human capital of individual leaders (their personal qualifications, skills and competencies), to developing their social capital (their ability to relate to others, their social skills and their emotional intelligence) (see Chapter 6). Thus, in line with greater appreciation of the relational qualities of effective leadership, Day reports a shift to a greater focus on building networks that encourage collaborations and cooperation. A decade later, leadership development scholars such as Turnbull James (2011) were arguing that since leadership is relational and collective in organisations, a focus on developing leaders will only have limited results and greater impact would be felt by taking an alternative approach that develops embedded processes and practices that engage all stakeholders, not just the people in leadership positions (see Chapter 4 on collective and distributed leadership).

PERSPECTIVES FROM PRACTICE 9.1

Priyanka Thali is a managing editor at CACTUS Communications, a technology company headquartered in India. More information about Priyanka can be found on page 3.

Ken Lorenz is the owner of a data analytics firm and a data analytics consultancy, both based in the USA. More information about Ken can be found on page 2.

Victor Ikande is a regional head for the US-based construction firm Hollins. More information about Victor can be found on page 3.

Claire McCarthy is the Director of Operations and HR at a large children's charity in Wales. More information about Claire can be found on page 2.

Priyanka Thali has been on various development courses in her leadership journey, including one that applied the DISC methodology (as referenced above). She claims:

> It was quite insightful in terms of raising my self-awareness. And I think self-awareness is so important when you're leading people. So it helped with that to some extent. It validated a lot of things that I thought about my own style and it also gave me a clearer picture and helped me identify things that I didn't necessarily know or think about. I have been on other courses and these have helped me: time management, for instance, stress management.

We have these sessions periodically and you can sign up for them, and I think because I continue to take these sessions even though I have been a manager for a little while, for me they serve as a validation of what I am already doing, and give me insights on what I should modify. So I think they are useful to me.

Priyanka also refers to other means by which she has developed as a leader, though: 'A lot of what I learned was from colleagues as things went along. The role itself kept evolving over the years and the structure kept evolving so a lot of what we learned was through experience, through talking to each other.'

Both Ken Lorenz and Victor Ikande identified that their approach to leading had been heavily influenced by a mentor. Victor explains his experience thus:

I had for nine years the privilege of a strong mentor. An honest gentleman who helped me shape my career and helped me understand what my strengths are. And he gave me guidance at the early stage. I think it was critical. I think that was the single biggest factor. Even now I mean when I get into deep water I have 'What would Dave do?' moments, you know, when I'm about to make a big decision.

Claire McCarthy articulates the downside of not being mentored or feeling supported: 'I struggle with leadership when you don't have the support of your leaders or your contemporaries, you know, the other leaders. I look for camaraderie, I look for support from my peers and I really struggle when I don't get it.'

Perspectives from practice questions

1. What types of training and leadership development do you think worked best for Priyanka?
2. What type of development do you think would work best for you in your organisation?
3. What value do you think Ken and Victor realised by having mentors?
4. Why do you think Claire finds it more difficult when she does not have support from her contemporaries and bosses?

Recent and current thinking about how to develop leadership in organisations includes the suggestion that in order to be most effective, leadership development might move away from *developing leaders* to *developing leadership*. This is informed by research that proposes and evidences leadership as a more holistic and distributed phenomenon in organisations (as explored in Chapter 4). To that end, Turnbull James and Ladkin (2008) propose that leadership development should involve leadership in context rather than just develop a set of generic skills. In particular, they outline the three key capabilities:

- perceiving – cognizance amongst personnel of themselves, others and the organisational context;
- interpreting – social awareness and experience of context and circumstances so as to shape embedded decisions and actions;
- connecting – competence in communicating and connecting with stakeholders within and external to the organisation.

Approaches to developing leadership that account for the wider organisation rather than just the career of the individual include coaching, scenario testing and simulation. Development techniques to these ends are still in their infancy and, though promising, the longer-term effects and scaleability of them are not yet fully known. In practice in many organisations in public, private and third sectors, leadership development and training still focus on those people who are in roles that require that they lead. However, current and emergent understanding about influence, the support of people, and the links between performance and motivations do inform how leadership may develop in organisations to include but also go beyond the individuals who may be trained and supported in leading roles. It is to some of these newest ideas about developing leadership, rather than leaders, in organisations that we turn to next.

DEVELOPING LEADERSHIP FOR THE FUTURE IN ORGANISATIONS

There has been much written about leadership development. This includes much work that outlines the various competencies that are important amongst leaders and various means by which these competencies might be achieved. Bennis and Thomas (2002) and Gill (2011), for example, stress the importance of experiences to inform practice, and while Gill outlines various means by which these experiences might be enabled (through task or role allocation, role models, etc.), Bennis and Thomas include also accidental and even traumatic learning experiences as constructive for developing leadership. Cunliffe (2009) adds that experiences may or may not be marked events; they include also the day-to-day small and incremental practices of organisational participation through which people learn by reflecting on these experiences and practices. As such, development occurs as a result of reflexive engagement of an individual with their circumstances, and it is this interaction that results in development of both people and the organisations they inhabit (see Chapter 4 on reflexivity). More recently, Harrison (2018) explains several key competencies that contribute to being an effective leader, including conceptual and creative skills and emotional intelligence and social skills, and recommends approaches that will enhance these.

In line with Cunliffe's focus on the importance of reflexivity, other studies show that leadership development is a protracted, continual process rather than the outcome of a training course (or indeed set of traits). Ford et al. (2008) asserts that our *implicit leadership theories* and an organisation's *leadership concept* (see Chapter 4) can act to limit the development of leadership for many. If people cannot perceive themselves as leaders because they do not conform in some way to the collectively identified ideal type, they may never step up. This implies a need for organisational boards and other leaders to interrogate their leadership structures and particularly the organisation's *leadership concept* in terms of effectiveness and whether it is acting to restrict, rather than enhance, the opportunities of leadership.

Elsewhere, some modern thinking about leadership development is questioning the appropriateness of developing individuals at all. First, research such as that of Raelin (2004) queries how effective developing skills in an individual can be if the people he or she will lead have had no such equivalent training. Further, research such as that of Bolden and Gosling (2006), Carroll et al. (2008) and Buchan (2019) exemplify an emerging school of thought that reasons that notions of leaders and leadership are rooted in experiences and models developed from knowledge of the past, and of course that past has subsequently been updated. Thus, these models are flawed since 1) they are based on incomplete understanding, and/or 2) they refer to an understanding of leading in a world that no longer exists – things have moved on, including the way people interact, their expectations, motivations, attitudes to work, etc. The testimonies of Jannie Tam, Claire McCarthy and Priyanka Thali in Chapter 7 evidence this in that each of these leaders identify that their approaches to younger people are modified in response to the different experiences and attitudes to life and work compared with previous generations. More generally, since social life broadly is not static, logic dictates that it is not reasonable to expect that what has worked in the past will work in the future, and indeed to model modern leadership development on past leadership experience will act only to replicate an organisation's leadership archetypes and *leadership concept*, including its inherent limitations, such as the hero stereotype and reliance on inequality.

Denyer and Turnbull James (2016) summarise the implications for organisations in terms of ongoing and future-oriented leadership development, as opposed to reliance on models of the past. These are that organisations should:

* interrogate and update where appropriate an organisation's *leadership concept*;
* focus on *what* is done to achieve effective leadership rather than who does it;
* explore leadership as embedded in an organisation's specific context and circumstances, with a focus on experiences and challenges specific to that organisation or sector, rather than view leadership as a generic concept;
* rather than focus on actions of leaders and followers as if they are discrete, appreciate that leadership is relational and focus on the development of relational approaches to leadership.

Despite these advancements in knowledge about developing leadership and proposed means by which leadership might better future-proof organisations, at a practical level, there is still much evidence of the development of leaders in organisations. As Boyce et al. (2010) note, present-day organisations do still experience improvement and enhancement as a result of having facilitated the development of leadership skills and abilities amongst those with potential for leadership/headship roles. It is to some of the key skills and approaches that support people to develop as leaders that we now turn.

Developing competencies in leading

In modern organisations, according to theory and knowledge explored throughout this book, there are various key things that make for effective leadership. These are myriad, complex and extensive, and, critically, they are context-specific and will vary depending on task, follower readiness, experience of the leader, circumstances of the organisation, position in the commercial or otherwise external environment, industry sector, and so on. That said, though, as the testimonies of the leaders featured throughout this book attest, there are also several overlapping and recurring themes. In this section, we will explore the development of skills and competencies for leading with reference to these general themes. These are extrapolated broadly as involving a leader's ability to:

- set clear aims or goals – the envisioning and *thought leadership* part of leading;
- connect with the team or other staff being led – implying the social and relational nature and demands of *leading people*;
- personalise the mission – implying an emotional investment on the part of the leader;
- lead by example – implying the personal responsibility requirements of being a leader.

While it is possible to summarise these components of effective leadership in this way, the key question that remains for many people who aspire to be leaders or aspire to improve their competence in leading is how to achieve these. There are countless books, manuals, websites, blog posts and videos available that claim to help improve leadership or develop leadership skills. Some of these resources are very useful – others not so much. Accessing role models, reading as much as possible and immersing oneself in available resources to be as informed as possible are all great ways to develop skills and abilities and build a body of knowledge for oneself. But it is important to engage critically. Not all resources are equal and some sources may be old-fashioned, not culturally appropriate for some circumstances or just not very good. Critique in and of itself can be helpful in developing knowledge in any case, as one can consider the usefulness and appropriateness of the content in the context of one's own experiences and expectations of organisations. So it is useful to explore widely the resources available but equally important:

- to engage critically;
- to consider the fit with your own organisational or social culture;
- to explore in particular your own industry or sector as these will be most relevant, but also look to analogous industries and explore whether there are lessons to be learnt from a wider pool of resources.

Throughout this book there are *implications for practice* extrapolated and *perspectives from practice* presented in each chapter. In addition, what follows is a summary that crystallises five of the recurrent and critical elements of effective leadership and makes suggestions about how one might advance these key skills so as to contribute to development of their ability to lead.

The five critical leadership competencies are: communicating, knowing, motivating, taking charge and representing. Each is considered in turn next.

1. Communicating

Communicating is relational. It is a two-way phenomenon, and knowledge is received and refined for everyone if a leader practices in both transmit and receive modes. Old-fashioned ideas about leadership position it as involving instructions from leader to followers in a one-directional way. Good leadership in modern organisations requires that communications are open and people are able to communicate ideas, opinions, expertise and concerns so as to contribute to and benefit organisational performance. It also allows that knowing (discussed later) can occur. Thus, some tips for communicating as a leader include the following:

- **Transmit clearly**

   Give clear instructions – people must be able to understand you and understand the goals you are trying to achieve. They must also be able to understand the value of these, so it can be important to explain why their work is important or how it fits into the value chain of the organisation.

   Convey enthusiasm – if the leader is not motivated, how can they expect anyone else to be? Leading requires communicating that the work being done is valuable, contributory and will lead to good or improved outcomes. This requires the expression of engagement and belief that this is the case.

   Express knowledge and confidence – a leader will be most effective where they are knowledgeable and inspire confidence in self and in the team. People should believe a leader is competent. This engenders trust in the leader and trust in the potential for good outcomes as a result of the work effort requested.

- **Receive well**

   Show interest – in the person and the ideas they may come to you with.

Be approachable – people will only communicate ideas and value if they are comfortable and trust that these will be received respectfully. It allows also that the leader can identify problems quickly and efficiently as a result of knowing (see later) the people he or she leads.

Personalise – use names, make eye contact. Where teams are large and it is not possible to be available for everyone, implement structures that do allow for personalised leading that has links to you or other leaders so that communications are enabled at scale.

Avoid a blame culture – in order to solicit good ideas and have people deliver information that is of use to a leader and an organisation, people must feel able to communicate with a leader in a safe way.

2. Knowing

Knowing people is important in terms of generating flows of information (facilitated by communicating well as above), and in terms of developing and maintaining trust. If people feel known and understood as individuals with their own tastes, desires, personality, experiences, background, etc., there is a greater chance of empathy and understanding between leader and follower. Motivation and engagement may be stimulated by considering people not as human resources but instead as human beings. On the other hand, knowing people also allows leaders to quickly identify those whose performance and effort is not good. Knowing people affords identifying whether this is a temporary blip in performance as a consequence of some life event perhaps, or whether it is of ongoing concern for the organisation. From this knowledge, remedial actions can be informed and indeed so can conversations about acceptability of effort and ongoing place (or not) in the organisation. In essence therefore, knowing might involve the following:

Knowing people – what makes them tick, what motivates them, what they are good at, what their ambitions are in the organisation and in their wide career.

Developing people – knowing where they have skills and experience gaps, knowing what they need in order to succeed.

Valuing people – engaging people so that they feel known and valued and part of the social and professional fabric of the organisation.

Understanding your assets – knowing people includes knowing about their explicit skills (from education or profession or training, including work-based and other types of skills such as dancing or cooking) and their tacit skills (their interests, their character, their personality). Knowing who is skilled at what – from finance skills to social and emotional intelligence – allows leaders to deploy people most effectively for the development of both follower and organisation.

3. Motivating

The purpose of leadership is to motivate people to perform in line with the objectives of the organisation (see Chapter 1 on motivations and the links with leadership). This is true of both *thought leadership* and *leading people. Thought leadership* therefore should be communicated with enthusiasm and clarity (as above), and it should inspire effort. *Leading people* should be similarly stimulating for people and encourage the development and maintenance of motivation. Some means by which this might be achieved are as follows:

Use praise – a key means of keeping people motivated is to praise when they do things well or when they add value.

Say thank you – possibly the most overlooked part of leading, but potentially the easiest and most effective. Too often this is missing in organisations and a lack of acknowledgement of effort is very demotivating.

Defer credit – linked to praising and thanking, a leader will motivate staff best when he or she gives credit where it is due. The purpose of extracting effort from people is to encourage their best performance, not to enhance the leader's profile.

Set attainable targets – nothing will demotivate people more than being told they are to achieve the impossible. Not only will this overburden, but there have to be achievements or people will believe that value is unattainable. The achievement of challenging but attainable goals motivates people to progress to the next targets and goals, and in turn this develops them and the performance of the organisation.

4. Taking charge

One of the key parts of leading people is to lead. This means taking responsibility and making decisions. Leaders may be directive or consultative or diplomatic or laissez faire, but when decisions have to be made, a leader has to make them. These decisions might rely on information and input from others, but ultimately the leader is responsible and the leader must lead. In organisations there is usually an expectation that leadership involves taking charge and because of this expectation people look to leaders to decide, plan, determine direction and approach and make judgements about what and how organisational goals and strategy will be operationalised. Of course, these also must be communicated clearly, as above. In practice, taking charge involves some of the following:

Being known – be known as the leader and set the structure and tone of how the team will operate.

Leading by example – a leader's conduct must be that which others might emulate. If a leader will not decide, act, conduct him/herself in a professional manner, no one else is likely to.

Being available – be available to receive ideas, opinions and field challenges and problems (facilitated by communications as above).

Being decisive – solicit opinions and knowledge where appropriate, but make decisions and take responsibility for those decisions.

5. Representing

A critical element of leading people is being their representative in the hierarchy. As noted throughout this book and in the testimonies of leaders, trust is central and vital to the ability to lead people effectively. Resonant with the ideals of servant leadership (see Chapter 3), if a leader is to engender trust amongst followers then he or she must be seen as championing and making good representation of them and must be trusted to support them and their activities. This is one of the elements of leadership most often missed from accounts of how to lead effectively, yet it is a critical part of establishing and maintaining trust between leaders and followers. Means by which representing people might be expressed include the following:

Being positive – represent your team in a positive light, focus on the value they add, the contribution they make to the overall departmental or organisational strategy or goals.

Avoiding blame **in** *the team* – where mistakes occur, avoid a blame culture. Not only does this support good communication of ideas and creativity (as outlined above), it also enables trust that a leader will not use scapegoats or punish genuine errors.

Avoiding blame **of** *the team* – a leader should strive to defend the position of his or her team relative to other teams or parts of the organisational structure.

Owning mistakes – the buck stops at a leader. If decisions and courses of action are determined by a leader (as per *taking charge* above), then errors of judgement or poor performance must be owned by that leader. This does not mean a leader should be penalised, but it does imply that effective leadership involves owning mistakes, not deferring them to someone else on the team, and, critically, taking the steps required to mitigate and correct performance problems.

PERSPECTIVES FROM PRACTICE 9.2

John Black is a station manager with one of the UK's fire and rescue services. More information about John can be found on page 2.

Jannie Tam is the founder of the Hong Kong-based talent development company GROWDynamics. More information about Jannie can be found on page 1.

Each participant leader who gave testimony for this book identified key parts of leading that they thought were the most important. These are described below. For each, there is clear resonance with the five 'best practice' tips given above.

John Black

You have to have realistic and achievable goals. And that is even at the highest strategic levels. If a goal is set that is unachievable then it makes it hard for all the leaders in the organisation to implement. You can't say the senior management is wrong, you have to support their messages, but you can't lead people with ridiculous objectives. It's the same when there is bad communication, where the strategy is not clear. That gets disseminated down, and then when a particular bit of strategy is not supported or properly understood, that filters down. Its all about the need for knowledge and experience and trust. And it's the same at all levels – you have to develop people and encourage them do things so they can actually succeed. So no impossible targets because they do more damage than good.

People will trust you if you are knowledgeable about your subject and you know what you are doing, and you can demonstrate that. There is always an opportunity to be able to reinforce the idea that there is an educated decision behind anything that they are asked to do, and they trust that. And that is built up just through knowledge and experience. If there's a point where there's a doubt in the knowledge of that triangle of knowledge, experience and trust, if people think that the knowledge isn't there, the whole thing falls apart.

Ken Lorenz

Like John, unattainable targets are also anathema to Ken in the private sector, and he claims communicating is the means by which leading is most effectively practised:

It's really hard to motivate someone who hates their job. Multiple times I have run into that situation where you can stand there with data and say, 'There's no way I can make this work. We don't have enough days in the quarter for the statistical model, it's mathematically impossible', and they're like, 'Well, just figure it out and get it done'. It's impossible. So it's about trying to find that common ground where you are saying, 'This is why we're all doing this. This is how we can build it and make it better. Just trying to build a better team and trying to build a group that all works for a common goal and sees the benefit'.

(Continued)

Claire McCarthy

Claire also claims communication is a critical element of leadership in the charity sector:

> Sell, don't tell. In my leading I've always had to change things. A big part of my working life is to make things more efficient, make things better. So I've always had to go in with kind of understanding that I'm about to change the way people are doing things. And people can resist change especially if they've been doing it for a long time. So I try and lead by speaking with them, collaborating with them, trying to get people to understand the benefit of change so they come with you. Trying to get them to see that while it might be a bit painful initially it's worth it in the long run. I don't like being too dictatorial with that because oftentimes especially if they've been doing it for a long time, they might have some knowledge about where in this process your idea might have a chink or not play well. Sometimes the people that are most resistant, the doubters, are the best ones to be around because they will point out flaws and then you can work around those flaws. So it's much better for outcomes if people come with you. If you can demonstrate a point and purpose to what you're trying to get them to do. That will make it successful.

Priyanka Thali

For Priyanka, knowledge is key, but there is also a paying forward element to her priorities for leading:

> I learned over a period of time that it is important to do your research and be able to have some sort of proof of concept, so people know you know what you are talking about and they trust that.

> The other things are that learning to pass on and empowerment are my main objectives. I believe that it's important to create independent thinkers. I want to know that I have harnessed people's talents and potential to their fullest. It's about passing forward, so tomorrow they also should be able to pass on to other people. I had one person and she was very dependent, very unsure of her decisions. She didn't want to do anything unless there was somebody telling her, 'OK, this is how you should go'. So with her my strategy was all about gradually getting her to think on her own. So every time she came to me with a problem or with something that she was not sure of, I tried to get her to do that thinking on her own and ask her, 'What do you think would work best?'. And then she would try and figure things out on her own and then we'd discuss it. Over a period of time, I have managed to foster some amount of ownership in this particular worker, so this person is a lot more self-reliant, turns to me a lot less and is also able to be a mentor of sorts to the other members of the team.

Jannie Tam

Jannie advocates ethics, inclusivity and treating people well as the most important elements of leadership in her small international business:

> For me it's all intrinsic. Extrinsic is important, but I think it is really important to have this intrinsic, more humanistic focus. It's about how you can still connect with people at a more heart to heart level. This is one of the benefits of working for a smaller company. We work with colleagues to actually co-create opportunities, so you know, colleagues consider it some form of progression.

Victor Ikande

For Victor, communications are important, especially the ability of people to contribute. He notes also that admitting and owning mistakes is a critical element in building trust and being able to lead effectively:

> Being able to speak freely and working in an environment that is psychologically safe for people to voice their opinions is absolutely essential. And on a number of occasions, I've made a mistake or the wrong move but acknowledged it was my decision as a leader. I've been in the position where that's happened, where a team member came up with something that they thought we should do. I thought differently about it but in the end I was wrong. And it was important that I went back to that person and acknowledged that if I had followed his opinion, it would have been better. I think it was important that there was a clear acknowledgement from my side, verbally, that I was wrong and he was right. And what I found was that that person became key in solving the problem ... he went over and above to fix it.

Perspectives from practice questions

1. Do you see any consistencies or differences in the testimonies from leaders regarding the things they claim are the most important for leading?
2. John and Priyanka both identify professional knowledge and competence as important for a leader. Do you agree that this is critical? Why/why not?
3. What do you think John or Ken might do to lead in circumstances they claim are limited by unattainable targets?
4. Why do you think people might resist change in the way Claire describes?
5. Do you think Claire's strategy of dealing with resistance is useful? What does she gain from it?
6. Jannie and Priyanka both highlight the value of developing and empowering people. What value do you think they realise from this?
7. Why does Victor stress the importance of 'safe psychological space'?
8. Why was it important that Victor admitted to a subordinate that he had made a mistake by not taking his advice?

SUMMARY

This chapter has explored the literature on leadership development and traced it from its roots of implementation in organisations through to the present-day challenges associated with developing leadership that will contribute to the organisations of the future. The chapter also summarises the principles in some of the myriad literature on how to develop leadership competencies and skills.

The central most critical element of leadership – whether referring to *thought leadership* or *leading people* – is trust. If a leader is trusted to come up with ideas and solutions, to plan, to strategise and to envision a different future, whether that involves paradigm shifts, commercial disruption or even just incremental change or strategic plans within a team, then those ideas need to be enabled. Equally, if a leader is trusted as competent to make informed decisions, respectful of other's opinions, engaged with the teams he or she leads, knowledgeable about their ambitions and sympathetic to their concerns, then that leader will be empowered to have the greatest influence on followers and their efforts in an organisation. Crystallised into two key principles, this chapter concludes with the assertion that effective leadership is that which seeks:

- *to contribute* and
- *to encourage and enable best efforts* from people.

The implication is that effective leadership involves a thought process that considers the organisational goals desired, the ambitions and motivations of the people one leads, and how the interests of each – organisation and people – can be aligned to realise value for both.

EXERCISES

Give an account of the evolving focus of leadership development over the last 75 years or so.

Give an explanation of why leadership development efforts in organisations have changed over time.

Reflect on your own organisation: what is the approach to leadership development there? Is it effective?

What do you consider might be appropriate ways of developing leaders to future-proof organisations in your industry or sector?

Consider your reflection from the exercise in Chapter 2 on your traits and abilities with regard to leadership. Do you hold the same view now?

What do you consider are your development needs to thrive in your organisations? What resources would you need for that?

Are leaders in your organisation trusted? If so, reflect on why; if not reflect on why not. What would you do to develop and establish trust in yourself as a leader?

CONCLUSION

Leadership is one of the important elements of organisational life. It is leadership that creates organisations and it is leadership that maintains them and makes the difference between those that succeed and those that don't. There are countless examples of the performance of organisations being attributed to the leadership of them. On any day of any week, in any place in the world, you will find reports in the media of leadership charged with having broken an organisation, rescued an organisation, maintained an organisation over a long or turbulent period, or even boosted an organisation's performance and impact. It's a fascinating and vital part of the milieu of organisational life.

Leading is complex, though. Leading in organisations in particular involves multiple stakeholders and requires consideration and reasoning. But, in fact, this is the purpose of leadership: to take the interests of many and manage them in such a way as to enable new ways of thinking or new ways of doing things. These are enabled by leadership. And it is leadership that will facilitate engagement amongst the people who will help in the realisation of ideas and achievement of goals, people who are supported to give their best level of participation and contribution. Leaders clearly therefore are not just born, they are made of informed, reflective and ethical conduct to which others may subscribe.

To conclude, the last words are reserved for Priyanka Thali and Claire McCarthy because they exhibit and crystallise both the challenges and the joys of leading in contemporary organisations:

> I want a team that is fully functional and reliable, that contributes to the organisations, a team that is happy doing what they are doing. My aim ultimately is to be able to lead a team of people who develop, people who will become the next, future leaders, but can have a life outside of work as well. (Priyanka)

> I work with compliance things – data protection, HR, health and safety – it's a lot of responsibility and it's not always easy. And staff can be challenging. But I wouldn't change it. Every day is different and every day I learn something new. (Claire)

ACKNOWLEDGEMENTS

I am very grateful to Jessica Moran and Ruth Stitt from Sage who have been so positive and constructive as I have prepared this book. I would also like to thank my lovely colleague Kate Sullivan, my lovely friend Nicolina Kamenou and her family, and my lovely sister Melissa Sutherland for helping me to source leaders to contribute their experiences. I would like to thank the participant leaders Priyanka Thali, Ken Lorenz, Jannie Tam and the three (Victor, Claire and John) who preferred to remain anonymous for giving their valuable time and telling me how things really are for them as leaders in organisations. Lastly, amongst the many, many reasons I have to say thank you to my husband, Neil Galloway, I have to add the fantastic support he's given me by helping to source participants, reading drafts, and commenting and critiquing throughout this process.

REFERENCES

Adams, J.S. (1963) Toward and understanding of inequity, *Journal of Abnormal and Social Psychology*, *67*, 422–436.

Alegbeleye, I. and Kaufman, E. (2020) Relationship between middle managers' transformational leadership and effective followership behaviors in organizations, *Journal of Leadership Studies*, *13*(4), 6–19.

Alimo-Metcalfe, B. and Alban-Metcalfe, R. (2001) The development of a new transformational leadership questionnaire, *Journal of Occupational and Organizational Psychology*, *74*(1), 1–27.

Andersson, J. (2020) Women's unpaid labour is worth £140bn to the UK economy, *INews*, 4 March.

Antonakis, J. (2012) Transformational and charismatic leadership. In D.V. Day and J. Antonakis (eds) *The Nature of Leadership*, pp. 256–288. Thousand Oaks, CA: Sage Publications.

Antonakis, J., Avolio, B.J. and Sivasubramaniam, N. (2003) Context and leadership: an examination of the nine-factor Full-Range Leadership Theory using the Multifactor Leadership Questionnaire, *The Leadership Quarterly*, *14*(3), 261–295.

Antonakis, J., Cianciolo, A.T. and Sternberg, R.J. (2004) Leadership: past, present, and future. In J. Antonakis, A.T. Cianciolo and R.J. Sternberg (eds) *The Nature of Leadership*, pp. 3–15. Thousand Oaks: Sage Publications.

Archer, M.S. (1998) Introduction: realism in the social sciences. In M.S. Archer R. Bhaskar, A. Collier et al. (eds) *Critical Realism: Essential Readings*, pp. 189–205. London: Routledge.

Avolio, B.J. (1999) *Full Leadership Development: Building the Vital Forces in Organizations*. Thousand Oaks, CA: Sage.

Avolio, B.J. and Bass, B.M. (2002) *Developing Potential across a Full Range of Leadership: Cases on Transactional and Transformational Leadership*. Mahwah, NJ: Lawrence Erlbaum Publishing.

Avolio, B.J. and Yammarino, F.J. (2013) *Transformational and Charismatic Leadership* (2nd edn). Bingley: Emerald Publishing.

Banu, S., Kamenou-Aigbekaen, N. and Galloway, L. (2020) A relational approach to exploring inequalities within the human resource management model in the Middle East, *International Journal of Work Organisation and Emotion*, *10*(2), 216–231.

Barnard, C.I. (1938) *The Functions of the Executive*. Cambridge, MA: Harvard University Press.

Barnett, A., Yandle, B. and Naufal, G. (2013) Regulation, trust, and cronyism in Middle Eastern societies: the simple economics of 'wasta', *Journal of Socio-Economics, 44*, 41–46.

Bass, B.M. (1985) *Leadership and Performance beyond Expectations*. New York: Free Press.

Bass, B.M. (1998) *Transformational Leadership: Industry, Military, and Educational Impact*. Mawah, NJ: Lawrence Erlbaum.

Bass, B.M. and Avolio, B.J. (1990) *Transformational Leadership Development: Manual for the Multifactor Leadership Questionnaire*. Palo Alto, CA: Consulting Psychologists Press.

Bennis, W. (1984) The four competencies of leadership, *Training and Development Journal, 38*, 14–19.

Bennis, W. and Thomas, R. (2002) *Geeks and Geezers*. Boston, MA: Harvard Business School Press.

Blake, R.R. and Mouton, J.S. (1964) *The Managerial Grid III*. Houston, TX: Gulf Publishing Company.

Boin A., Hart P., Stern E. and Sudelius B. (2016) *Politics of Crisis Management: Public Leadership under Pressure*. New York: Cambridge University Press.

Bolden, R. and Gosling, J. (2006) Leadership competencies: time to change the tune? *Leadership, 2*(2), 147–163.

Boyce, L., Zaccaro, S. and Wisecarver, M. (2010) Propensity for self-development of leadership attributes: understanding, predicting, and supporting performance of leader self-development, *The Leadership Quarterly, 21*(1), 159–178.

Broodryk, J. (2005) *Ubuntu Management Philosophy: Exploring Ancient African Wisdom into the Global World*. Johannesburg: Knowles Publishing.

Brown, A.D. and Thornborrow, W.T. (1996) Do organisations get the followers they deserve? *Leadership and Organization Development Journal, 17*(1), 5–11.

Buchan, L. (2019) Leadership-as-communicative-practice: transforming situations through talk and text, unpublished PhD thesis, University of Strathclyde.

Burke, R. and Barron, S. (2007) *Project Management Leadership: Building Creative Teams*. Birmingham, MI: Burke Publishing.

Burns, I.M. (1978) *Leadership*. New York: Harper & Row.

Butler, J. (1990) *Gender Trouble: Feminism and the Subversion of Identity*. London: Routledge.

Carlyle, T. (1841) *On Heroes, Hero-Worship, and the Heroic in History*. London: James Fraser.

Carroll, B., Levy, L. and Richmond, D. (2008) Leadership as practice: challenging the competency paradigm. *The Leadership Quarterly, 4*(4), 363–379.

Cleland, D.I. (1995) Leadership and the project-management body of knowledge. *International Journal of Project Management, 13*(2), 83–88.

Crevani, L. (2019) Relational Leadership. In B. Carroll, J. Ford and S. Taylor (eds) *Leadership: Contemporary Critical Perspectives*. Thousand Oaks, CA: Sage Publications.

Crevani, L., Lindgren, M. and Packendorff, J. (2010) Leadership, not leaders: on the study of leadership as practices and interactions, *Scandinavian Journal of Management, 26,* 77–86.

Crossman, B. and Crossman, J. (2011) Conceptualising followership – a review of the literature, *Leadership, 7*(4), 481–497.

Cunliffe, A. (2009) The philosophical leader: on relationalism, ethics and reflexivity – a critical perspective to teaching leadership, *Management Learning, 40*(1), 87–101.

Day, D. (2001) Leadership development: a review in context, *The Leadership Quarterly, 11*(4), 581–613.

Denis, J.L., Langley, A. and Sergi, V. (2012) Leadership in the plural, *The Academy of Management Annals, 6*(1), 211–283.

Denyer, D. and Turnbull James, K. (2016) Doing leadership-as-practice development. In J.A. Raelin (ed.) *Leadership-as-Practice: Theory and Application,* pp. 262–283. New York: Routledge.

DeRue, D.S., Nahrgang, J.D., Wellman, N. and Humphrey, S.E. (2011) Trait and behavioral theories of leadership: an integration and meta-analytic test of their relative validity, *Personnel Psychology, 64,* 7–52.

Douglas, M. (1970) *Natural Symbols.* London: Barrie & Rockliff.

Dowd, M. (2018) Lady of the rings: Jacinda rules, *The New York Times,* 8 September.

Drath, W.H., McCauley, C.D., Palus, C.J., Van Velsor, E., O'Connor, P.M.G. and McGuire, J.B. (2008) Direction, alignment, commitment: toward a more integrative ontology of leadership, *The Leadership Quarterly, 19*(6), 635–653.

Dvir, T. and Shamir, B. (2003) Follower developmental characteristics as predicting transformational leadership: a longitudinal field study, *The Leadership Quarterly, 14*(3), 327–344.

Eagly, A.H. (1987) *Sex Differences in Social Behavior: A Social-Role Interpretation.* Hillsdale, NJ: Erlbaum.

Eagly, A.H. (2005) Achieving relational authenticity in leadership: does gender matter? *The Leadership Quarterly, 16*(3), 459–474.

Eagly, A.H., Nater, C., Miller, D.I., Kaufmann, M. and Sczesny, S. (2020) Gender stereotypes have changed: a cross-temporal meta-analysis of U.S. public opinion polls from 1946 to 2018, *American Psychologist, 75*(3), 301–315.

Eagly, A.H. and Wood, W. (2012) Social role theory. In P. van Lange, A. Kruglanski and E.T. Higgins (eds) *Handbook of Theories in Social Psychology,* pp. 458–476. Thousand Oaks, CA: Sage Publications.

Eagly, A. H. and Wood, W. (2013) The nature–nurture debates: 25 years of challenges in understanding the psychology of gender. *Perspectives on Psychological Science, 8*(3), 340–357.

Earley, P.C. and Ang, S. (2003) *Cultural intelligence: Individual Interactions across Cultures.* Palo Alto, CA: Stanford University Press.

Ferrer-Pérez, V.A. and Bosch-Fiol, E. (2014) The measure of the masculinity–femininity construct today: some reflections on the case of the Bem Sex Role Inventory. *International Journal of Social Psychology, 29*(1), 180–207.

Fiedler, F.E. (1967) *A Theory of Leadership Effectiveness*. New York: McGraw-Hill.

Fiedler, F.E. (1995) 'Reflections by an accidental theorist', *Leadership Quarterly*, 6(4), 453–461.

Fitzsimons, D. (2016) How shared leadership changes our relationships at work, *Harvard Business Review*, 12 May.

Florida, R. (2003) Entrepreneurship, creativity and regional economic growth. In D.M. Hart (ed.) *The Emergence of Entrepreneurship Policy: Governance, Start-ups and Growth in the US Knowledge Economy*. Cambridge: Cambridge University Press.

Ford, J., Harding, N. and Learmonth, M. (2008) *Leadership as Identity: Constructions and Deconstructions*. Basingstoke: Palgrave Macmillan.

Friede, G., Busch, T. and Bassen, A. (2015) ESG and financial performance: aggregated evidence from more than 2000 empirical studies, *Journal of Sustainable Finance & Investment*, 5(4), 210–233.

Galloway, L. and Haniff, A. (2015) Managing projects in architecture: a study of leadership in a creative industry. *Open Economics and Management Journal*, 2(1), 38–44.

Galloway, L., Kapasi, I. and Sang, K. (2015) Entrepreneurship, leadership and the value of feminist approaches to understanding them. *Journal of Small Business Management*, 53(3), 693–692.

Galloway, L., Sanders, J. and Keogh, W. (2009) Leadership and growth in entrepreneurial firms. In J.E. Michaels and L.F. Piraro (eds) *Small Business: Innovation, Problems and Strategy*. Hauppauge, NY: Nova Science Publishers.

Gardner, W.L., Avolio, B.J., Luthans, F., May, D.R. and Walumbwa, F.O. (2005) Can you see the real me? A self-based model of authentic leader and follower development. *Leadership Quarterly*, 16, 343–372.

Gibson-Graham, J.K. (2008) Diverse economies: performative practices for other worlds. *Progress in Human Geography*, 32(5), 613–632.

Gill, R. (2011) *Theory and Practice of Leadership*. London: Sage.

Gipson, A.N., Pfaff, D.L., Mendelsohn, D.B., Catenacci, L.T. and Burke, W.W. (2017) Women and leadership: selection, development, leadership style, and performance, *The Journal of Applied Behavioral Science*, 53(1), 32–65.

Goleman, D. (1998a) *Working with Emotional Intelligence*. New York: Bantam.

Goleman, D. (1998b) What makes a leader? *Harvard Business Review*, 76(6), 93–103.

Goleman, D. (2000) Leadership that gets results, *Harvard Business Review*, 78, 78–90.

Graen, G.B. (2006) In the eye of the beholder: cross-cultural lesson in leadership from project GLOBE, *Academy of Management Perspectives*, 20, 95–101.

Graen, G.B. and Uhl-Bien, M. (1995) The relationship-based approach to leadership: development of LMX theory of leadership over 25 years: applying a multi-level, multi-domain perspective. *Leadership Quarterly*, 6(2), 219–247.

Grant Thornton (2021) *Women in Business 2021*, available at http://grantthorntonglobal.com.

Guo, Y., Rammal, H.G., Benson, J. Zhu, Y. and Dowling, P.J. (2018) Interpersonal relations in China: expatriates' perspective on the development and use of guanxi, *International Business Review, 27*(2), 455–464.

Handy, C. (1993) *Understanding Organisations* (4th edn). London: Penguin.

Harrison, C. (2018) *Leadership Theory and Research: A Critical Approach to New and Existing Paradigms*. London: Palgrave Macmillan.

Hersey, P. and Blanchard, K.H. (1969) Life cycle theory of leadership, *Training and Development Journal, 23*(5), 26–34.

Hersey, P. and Blanchard, K.H. (1977) *Management of Organizational Behavior: Utilizing Human Resources* (3rd edn). Englewood Cliffs, NJ: Prentice-Hall.

Hersey, P. and Blanchard, K.H. (1982) Leadership style: attitudes and behaviours, *Training and Development Journal, 36*(5), 50–52.

Herzberg, F. (1966) *Work and Nature of Man*. Cleveland, OH: World Publishing Company.

HESA (Higher Education Statistics Agency) (2021) *What Do HE Students Study?* 2019–2020 data, available at www.hesa.ac.uk/data-and-analysis/students/what-study.

Hofstede, G. (1980) *Culture's Consequences: International Differences in Work-Related Values*. Beverly Hills, CA: Sage.

Hofstede, G. (1991) *Cultures and Organizations: Software of the Mind*. London: McGraw-Hill.

Hofstede, G. (2001) *Culture's Consequences: Comparing Values, Behaviors, Institutions and Organizations across Nations*. Thousand Oaks, CA: Sage.

Hofstede, G. (2011) Dimensionalizing cultures: the Hofstede model in context. *Online Readings in Psychology and Culture, 2*(1).

Hofstede, G. and Bond, M.H. (1988) The Confucius connection: from cultural roots to economic growth. *Organizational Dynamics, 16*(4), 5–21.

House, R.J. (1971) A path–goal theory of leadership effectiveness. *Administrative Science Quarterly, 16*(3), 321–328.

House, R.J. (1977) A 1976 theory of charismatic leadership. In J.G. Hunt and L.L. Larson (eds) *Leadership: The Cutting Edge*. Carbondale, IL: Southern Illinois University Press.

House, R.J., Dorfman, P.W., Javidan, M., Hanges, P.J. and Sully de Luque, M.F. (2013) *Strategic Leadership across Cultures: The GLOBE Study of CEO Leadership Behavior and Effectiveness in 24 Countries*. Thousand Oaks, CA: Sage Publications.

House, R.J., Hanges, P.J., Javidan, M., Dorfman, P.W. and Gupta, V. (2004) *Culture, Leadership, and Organizations: The GLOBE Study of 62 Societies*. Thousand Oaks, CA: Sage Publications.

Howell, J. and Avolio, B. (1992) The ethics of charismatic leadership: submission or liberation? *The Academy of Management Executive, 6*(2), 43–54.

Hundley, G. (2000) Male/female earnings differences in self-employment: the effects of marriage, children, and the household division of labour, *Industrial and Labor Relations Review, 54*(1), 95–114.

Jepson, D. (2009) Studying leadership at cross-country level: a critical analysis, *Leadership, 5*(1), 61–80.

Jin, Y. (2010) Emotional leadership as a key dimension of public relations leadership: a national survey of public relations leaders, *Journal of Public Relations Research, 22*(2), 159–181.

Joy, L., Carter, N.M., Wagener, H.M. and Narayanan, S. (2007) *The Bottom Line: Corporate Performance and Women's Representation on Boards*. New York: Catalyst.

Kapasi, I., Sang, K. and Sitko, R. (2016) Gender, authentic leadership and identity: analysis of women leaders' autobiographies, *Gender in Management: An International Journal, 31*(5/6), 339–358.

Katz, R.L. (1955) Skills of an effective administrator, *Harvard Business Review, 33*(1), 33–42.

Keegan, P. (2015) Here's what really happened at that company that set a $70,000 minimum wage, *INC Magazine*, November.

Kelley, R.E. (1988) In praise of followers, *Harvard Business Review, 66*(6), 142–148.

Kort, E. (2008) What, after all, is leadership? 'Leadership' and plural action, *Leadership Quarterly 19*(4), 409–425.

Kotter, J.P. (1990) *A Force for Change: How Leadership Differs from Management*. New York: The Free Press.

Kouzes, J. and Posner, B. (2012) *The Leadership Challenge: How to Make Extraordinary Things Happen in Organisations*. San Francisco, CA: Jossey-Bass.

Ladkin, D. (2019) Leadership, management and headship. In B. Carroll, J. Ford and S. Taylor (eds) *Leadership: Contemporary Critical Perspectives*. Thousand Oaks, CA: Sage.

Laguda, E. (2021) Toxic leadership: managing its poisonous effects on employees and organizational outcomes. In S. Dhiman (ed.) *The Palgrave Handbook of Workplace Well-Being*, pp. 969–999. Cham, Switzerland: Palgrave Macmillan.

Langowitz, N. and Minniti, M. (2007) The entrepreneurial propensity of women, *Entrepreneurship, Theory and Practice, 31*(3), 341–364.

Locke, E.A. and G.P. Latham (1990) *A Theory of Goal Setting and Task Performance*. Englewood Cliffs, NJ: Prentice Hall.

Lord, R.C., DeVader, C.L. and Alliger, G.M. (1986) A meta-analysis of the relation between personality traits and leadership perceptions: an application of validity generalization procedures, *Journal of Applied Psychology, 71*(3), 402–410.

Manz, C.C., Shipper, F. and Stewart, G.L. (2009) Everyone a team leader: shared influence at W. L. Gore & Associates. *Organizational Dynamics, 38*, 239–244.

Maslow, A.H. (1954) *Motivation and Personality*. New York, Harper & Row.

McClelland, D.C. (1985) *Human Motivation*. Glenview, IL: Scott Foresman.

McCrae, R.R. (2008) Interpreting GLOBE Societal Practices Scales, *Journal of Cross-Cultural Psychology, 39*, 805–810.

McGregor, D. (1960) *The Human Side of Enterprise*. New York: McGraw-Hill.

McKinsey & Co and LeanIn (2020) Women in the Workplace, McKinsey & Co, available at https://wiw-report.s3.amazonaws.com/Women_in_the_Workplace_2020.pdf.

McSweeney B. (2002) Hofstede's model of national cultural differences and their consequences: a triumph of faith – a failure of analysis, *Human Relations, 55*(1), 89–118.

Mesinioti, P., Angouri, J., O'Brien, S., Bristowe, K. and Siassakos, D. (2020) 'Get me the airway there': negotiating leadership in obstetric emergencies. *Discourse & Communication*, *14*(2), 150–174.

Miles, R.E. and Snow, C.C. (1978) *Organizational Strategy, Structure and Process*. New York: McGraw-Hill.

Minkov, M. (2011) *Cultural Differences in a Globalizing World*. Bingley: Emerald.

Minkov, M. and Hofstede G. (2012) Hofstede's fifth dimension: new evidence from the World Values Survey, *Journal of Cross-Cultural Psychology*, *43*(1), 3–14.

Mintzberg, H. and Waters, J.A. (1985) Of strategies, deliberate and emergent. *Strategic Management Journal*, *6*(3), 257–272.

Mirchandani, K. (1999) Feminist insight on gendered work: new directions in research on women and entrepreneurship, *Gender, Work and Organization*, *6*(4), 224–235.

Mullangi, S. and Jagsi, R. (2019) Imposter syndrome: treat the cause, not the symptom, *Journal of the American Medical Association*, *322*(5), 403–404.

Müller, R. and Turner, J.R. (2007) Matching the project manager's leadership style to project type, *International Journal of Project Management*, *25*(1), 21–32.

Müller, R. and Turner, R. (2010) Leadership competency profiles of successful project managers, *International Journal of Project Management*, *28*(5), 437–448.

Mumford, M.D., Zaccaro, S.J., Harding, F.D., Jacobs, T.O. and Fleishman, E.A. (2000) Leadership skills for a changing world: solving complex social problems, *Leadership Quarterly*, *11*(1), 11–35.

Nassar, C., Nastacă, C.C. and Nastaseanu, A. (2021) The leadership styles of men and women—has the perception regarding female leaders changed? *Journal of US–China Public Administration*, *18*(2), 68–80.

Newenham-Kahindi, A. (2009) The transfer of Ubuntu and Indaba business models abroad: a case of South African multinational banks and telecommunication services in Tanzania, *International Journal of Cross Cultural Management*, *9*(1), 87–108.

O'Boyle Jr, E.H., Humphrey, R.H., Pollack, J.M., Hawyer, T.H. and Story, P.A. (2010) The relation between emotional intelligence and job performance: a meta-analysis. *Journal of Organizational Behavior*, *22*(5), 788–818.

Padilla, A., Hogan, R. and Kaiser, R.B. (2007) The toxic triangle: destructive leaders, susceptible followers and conducive environments, *The Leadership Quarterly*, *18*(3), 176–194.

Paustian-Underdahl, S.C., Walker, L.S. and Woehr, D.J. (2014) Gender and perceptions of leadership effectiveness: a meta-analysis of contextual moderators, *Journal of Applied Psychology*, *99*, 1129–1145.

Pearce, C.L. and Conger, J.A. (2003) *Shared Leadership: Reframing the Hows and Whys of Leadership*. Thousand Oaks, CA: Sage Publications.

Pedersen, L.H., Fitzgibbons, S. and Pomorski, L. (2021) Responsible investing: the ESG-efficient frontier, *Journal of Financial Economics*, *142*(2), 572–597.

Place, K.R. and Vardeman-Winter, J. (2018) Where are the women? An examination of research on women and leadership in public relations, *Public Relations Review*, *44*(1), 165–173.

Porter, M. (1990) *The Competitive Advantage of Nations*. London: Macmillan.

Porter, M.E. (1985) *Competitive Advantage*. New York: Free Press.

Post, C. and Byron, K. (2015) Women on boards and firm financial performance: a meta-analysis, *The Academy of Management Journal*, *58*(5), 1546–1571.

Potter, E. and Rosenbach, W. (2006) Followers as partners: the spirit of leadership. In W. Rosenbach and R. Taylor (eds) *Contemporary Issues in Leadership*. Boulder, CO: Westview Press.

Prabhakar, G.P. (2005) Switch leadership in projects: an empirical study reflecting the importance of transformational leadership on project success across twenty-eight nations. *Project Management Journal*, *36*(4), 53–60.

Probert, J. and Turnbull James, K. (2011) Leadership development: crisis, opportunities and the leadership concept. *Leadership*, *7*(2), 137–150.

Raelin, J. (2004) Don't bother putting leadership into people, *Academy of Management Executive*, *18*, 131–135.

Raelin, J. (2021) Action learning as a human resource development resource to realize collective leadership, *Human Resource Development Review*, *20*(3), 282–288.

Rowe, W.G. (2001) Creating wealth in organisations: the role of strategic leadership. *Academy of Management Review*, *15*(1), 81–94.

Salih, A.M. (2020) *Cross-Cultural Leadership: Being Effective in an Era of Globalization, Digital Transformation and Disruptive Innovation*. London: Routledge.

Schoemaker, P.J.H., Heaton, S. and Teece, D. (2018) Innovation, dynamic capabilities, and leadership, *California Management Review*, *61*(1), 15–42.

Shamir, B., House, R. and Arthur, M. (1993) The motivational effects of charismatic leadership: a self-concept based theory', *Organization Science*, *4*(4), 577–594.

Shanahan, R., Rosen, B., Schofer, J., Siler Fisher, A., Wald, D., Weiner, S., Boles, S., Ali Cheaito, M., Bond, M.C. and Kazzi, A. (2020) Medical student leadership in emergency medicine, *The Journal of Emergency Medicine*, *58*(5), 233–235.

Shenhar, A.J. (2004) Strategic project leadership: toward a strategic approach to project management. *R&D Management*, *34*(5), 569–578.

Simionescu, L.N., Gherghina, S.C. and Tawil, H. (2021) Does board gender diversity affect firm performance? Empirical evidence from Standard & Poor's 500 Information Technology Sector. *Financial Innovation*, *7*, online first, available at https://jfin-swufe.springeropen.com/track/pdf/10.1186/s40854-021-00265-x.pdf

Steele, C.M. (1997) A threat in the air: how stereotypes shape intellectual identity and performance. *American Psychologist*, *52*(6), 613–629.

Stogdill, R.M. (1948) Personal factors associated with leadership: a survey of the literature. *Journal of Psychology*, *25*, 35–71.

Stogdill, R.M. (1974) *Handbook of Leadership*. New York: Free Press.

Stogdill, R.M. and Coons, A.E. (1957) Leader behavior: its description and measurement. Research Monograph Number 88, Ohio State University Bureau of Business Research.

Syed, J. and Ozbilgin, M. (2019) *Managing Diversity and Inclusion: An International Perspective*. London: Sage.

Tayeb, M. (2001) Conducting research across cultures: overcoming drawbacks and obstacles. *International Journal of Cross Cultural Management*, *1*(1), 91–108.

Tracey, J.B. and Hinkin, T.R. (1998) Transformational leadership or effective managerial practices? *Group & Organization Management*, *23*(3), 220–236.

Turnbull James, K. (2011) *Leadership in Context: Lessons from New Leadership Theory and Current Leadership Development Practice*. London: The King's Fund.

Turnbull James, K. and Burgoyne, J. (2001) *Leadership Development: Best Practice Guide for Organisations*. London: Council for Excellence in Management and Leadership.

Turnbull James, K. and Ladkin, D. (2008) Meeting the challenge of leading in the 21st century: beyond the 'deficit' model of leadership development. In K. Turnbull James and J. Collins (eds) *Leadership Learning: Knowledge into Action*. Basingstoke: Palgrave Macmillan.

Uhl-Bien, M. and Ospina, S. (2012) *Advancing Relational Leadership*. Charlotte, NC: Information Age Publishing.

Uhl-Bien, M., Riggio, R.E., Lowe, K.B. and Carsten, M.K. (2014) Followership theory: a review and research agenda, *The Leadership Quarterly*, *25*(1), 83–104.

UN (United Nations) (2021) *Universal Declaration of Human Rights*, available at www.un.org/en/about-us/universal-declaration-of-human-rights.

UN Sustainable Development Group (2021) *Agenda 2030*, available at https://unsdg.un.org/2030-agenda/universal-values.

UN Women (2021) Facts and figures: women's leadership and political participation, available at www.unwomen.org.

UNESCO (United Nations Educational, Scientific and Cultural Organization) (2020) *Global Education Report 2020*, available at https://unesdoc.unesco.org/ark:/48223/pf0000374514.

United Nations Strategic Development Goals (2015) Available at www.un.org/sustainable development/.

Urban Dictionary (2021) Available at www.urbandictionary.com.

Venaik, S. and Brewer, P. (2013) Critical issues in the Hofstede and GLOBE national culture models, *International Marketing Review*, *30*(5), 469–482.

Vroom, V.H. (1964) *Work and Motivation*. New York: Wiley.

Walumbwa, F.O., Avolio, B.J., Gardner, W.L., Wernsing, T.S. and Peterson, S.J. (2008) Authentic leadership: development and validation of a theory-based measure, *Journal of Management*, *34*(1), 89–126.

Waugh W.L. (2018) Leadership and emergency management. In A. Farazmand (eds) *Global Encyclopedia of Public Administration, Public Policy, and Governance*. New York: Springer.

Weber, M. (1930) *The Protestant Ethic and the Spirit of Capitalism*, English translation of *Die Protestantische Ethik und der Geist des Kapitalismus* (1905), London: Allen & Unwin.

WEF (World Economic Forum) (2020) The Global Risks Report 2020, available at www.weforum.org/reports/the-global-risks-report-2020.

Yukl, G. (1993) A retrospective on Robert House's '1976 theory of charismatic leadership' and recent revisions, *The Leadership Quarterly*, 4(3–4), 367–373.

Yukl, G. (2010) *Leadership in Organizations*. Upper Saddle River, NJ: Pearson Education Ltd.

Zenger, J. and Folkman, J. (2019) Women score higher than men in most leadership skills, *Harvard Business Review*, June, available at https://hbr.org/2019/06/research-women-score-higher-than-men-in-most-leadership-skills

INDEX